Pray With Your Dogma

Pray With Your Dogma
Discover the spiritual energy of love!

Garrett Walker

Published by Woodland Creative Publishing

This book is an invitation to embark on a journey of discovery, where you'll uncover the divine in the simplest moments—like sitting with a dog at your feet. Through heartfelt reflections, you'll explore how love is the force that creates, unites, and manifests in all forms of life.

Published by Woodland Creative Publishing

Website: www.PrayWithYourDogma.com

Paperback ISBN: 979-8-218-60291-8

This book is a work of nonfiction. The views expressed are those of the author and do not necessarily reflect those of the publisher.

This book contains original text and artwork by the author. Most illustrations are AI-assisted graphic interpretations derived from the author's original photographs and refined using Photoshop. The back cover image was AI-generated based on a conceptual description and further adjusted by the author to align with the book's artistic vision.

Printed in the United States of America

First Edition

DEDICATION

To my dog and best friend, Honey Bear.

I began writing this book on Honey Bear's 12th birthday, which, unbeknownst to me, would also be her last. Looking back, I believe starting on her birthday was no mere coincidence but a moment of divine inspiration.

Honey Bear's love and companionship connected me with God in ways I had never known before. Her presence reminded me of the profound truth that love is the essence of the divine, uniting us in spirit.

And so, I dedicate this book to Honey Bear, my sweet baby girl, whose love continues to inspire me. She taught me to see the divine in the everyday and to know that we are one in spirit, forever connected.

To my dearest friend Cindy Lou
For over forty years we've shared the love and care for
our dogs Woody, Sheena, Honey and Casper.
Without you, and our dogs, my journey to discover
true love would not have been possible and
this book would never have happened.

PRAY WITH YOUR DOG

PREFACE

T his book is the culmination of a five-year journey—a journey that began as I sat quietly with my dog, pondering the simple yet profound energy of love flowing between us. What started as curiosity grew into a deeper exploration of the nature of God and the boundless spiritual truths that connect us all.

The first two chapters explore questions about the nature of love. The third chapter opens the door to profound spiritual discoveries of God and creation. I started to think about the building blocks of life—atoms made of particles held together by a mysterious energy force. I wondered, what if that mysterious force is the very same spiritual energy of love I was feeling in those quiet moments? This idea planted a seed that grew into a deeper understanding: everything in existence is both material and spiritual, and love is that spiritual energy that unites them.

Through this lens, I began to see God not as a distant entity but as the infinite spiritual energy that binds all things, manifesting in endless material forms. We and everything around us are expressions of one divine spirit, evolving freely in a dance of creation. God, I realized, is love itself—a force that delights in creation and experiences it through infinite evolutionary manifestations.

This journey also revealed the importance of balance. In our material existence, it is easy to become consumed by extreme desires that pull us out of harmony--*like becoming so driven by financial interests we lose touch with family & friends*. Yet through prayer and meditation, we can reconnect with our spiritual purpose, aligning our material lives with the moral guidance of love--*like reminding ourselves material comforts are empty without personal relationships*.

This book is about that balance—about understanding that our material selves are not separate from the divine. We are, in fact, God manifesting in infinite, evolving forms. It's about living with intention, guided by spiritual moral purpose, and realizing that the energy we call love is the very essence of God. Through love, we are united as one in all of creation, embodying the divine within ourselves and in everything that exists.

I also came to realize that heaven is not some distant, future place we must wait for. Heaven is all around us, here and now. It is not something we must seek; it is something we must see. When we live in alignment with our divine purpose—guided by love and spiritual intention—we awaken to the truth that we are already experiencing the wonder of heaven. It is eternal, and so are we. By living our best lives, we come to see that heaven is not something we will someday enter; it is something we are eternally a part of.

Perhaps the most surprising revelation for me was this: 'Love', *not consciousness*, is the true mystery of existence. Love is actually a spiritual energy that binds all particles of matter. It's like a divine force that fuels everything. Also Love is the only emotion: all other feelings are a result, or an expression of love-*like, happiness is a result of love, whereas sadness is losing love.* On the other hand, contrary to common thought, 'consciousness' acts like a lens, focusing decisions and actions tailored to individual purposes. So, while Love is the driving energy of evolutionary creation that creates both me and my dog, the differences in our conscious abilities are limited to address the unique needs of our purposes.

And what has amazed me the most is that these truths didn't come to me through books or formal study. They were revealed through quiet reflection, prayer, and a sense of inner knowing. Later, I discovered these ideas mirrored in theology, philosophy, and even science, affirming their resonance. This taught me that anyone with a sincere heart and the courage to seek can uncover the same truths. As scripture reminds us, "Seek, and ye shall find."

This book is not meant to be a theological argument or a philosophical treatise. It is a journey—a path that led me to profound spiritual awakenings and a clearer understanding of God. My hope is that it will encourage you to embark on your own journey of discovery, to seek God in the everyday moments, and to feel the presence of divine love in your life.

Ultimately, finding God is a personal experience, as unique as each of us. It doesn't require expertise or specific knowledge, only an open heart and a willingness to seek. As you begin this journey, I invite you to reflect on one simple truth that has become clear to me: **Love is God, and through love, we are one.**

So, wherever you are and however you choose to begin, may you find the infinite spirit of love in the quiet moments of life. Perhaps even in the company of a faithful dog at your feet. *My humble suggestion...* ***"Pray with your dog!"***

CHAPTER ONE

Sitting

WITH MY DOG

LOOK DEEP
INTO NATURE!

1 | SITTING WITH MY DOG

Einstein said,
"Look deep into nature, then you will
understand everything better."

My interest in writing about this began with me sitting quietly with my dog and asking myself, "Is she thinking, or just experiencing?" In that moment, I found myself pondering the profound simplicity of her world and the way it contrasted with the complexities of mine. What began as a quiet reflection turned into a deeper exploration of mindfulness, love, and divine connection.

We all know the peace we feel when taking a walk or sitting with our dog—those precious moments of escape from the busyness of life. For a few minutes, we can forget about the world and become more aware of the little things around us: nature, fresh air, blue sky, birds singing. But then there are the not-so-natural things: my neighbor mowing his grass, another neighbor washing his car, an Amazon driver delivering packages. These distractions pull me back into my mind's endless chatter—the things I need to take care of, calls I need to make, obligations waiting for me.

Recognizing those distractions, I turn my attention back to my dog and try to focus on what she's thinking. Her experience must be so different from mine. She notices the fresh air, the blue sky, the birds singing. She hears the neighbor mowing, but to her, it's just sound—no concept of "what" or "why". She sees the man washing his car but doesn't know what a car is or understand anything about the responsibilities of owning them. They're just things that are there, and the human is doing something. The Amazon driver? Just another person moving back and forth. She doesn't know about the internet or buying things—only that this man sometimes gives her a treat. And unlike me, she's not thinking about what's next or what needs to get done. She's just here, now, fully present. For her, this moment is all that matters.

I find myself drawn deeper into her reality, wanting to experience her state of mind. What if I could "mind meld" with her for just five minutes? I imagine it would be overwhelming—the sights, sounds, and smells she perceives, the fullness of the moment without the distractions of analysis or planning. This realization increases my awareness of the clutter in my own thoughts, blocking me from experiencing the richness of this moment. So I try to let go—to expel the busyness from my brain and focus only on her. I try to forget everything else and to meditate on her experience.

What is she feeling right now?

For me to fully grasp her state of mind I need to tell myself this moment is the most important thing I will do today. I need to identify the mental chatter running through my mind and try to set it all aside. And then let go of my worries, obligations, my job, my phone, my car, my to-do list. I tell myself the world can do without me for a while. Letting go of everything, I take a deep breath of fresh air, look again at the sky, and realize how small all the 'doings' of my life are in relation to the vastness of creation. I ask myself: What if this moment is all I will ever have? How would I live it? What would I do? Would I pray?

I think I would simply breathe in the wonder of everything around me, feeling all the blessings of love that have touched my life in this one last moment.

So, I look again at my dog lying here. I meditate on what she must be thinking and realize her natural experience is already in the space where I've been working to bring my own awareness. She simply lives in this moment, untouched by the busy chaos of the world. She's just taking it all in.

Dogs' senses are so much more attuned to the world than ours. Like how their world is shaped so much more by smell. When we smell vegetable soup, they smell each individual vegetable. A dog's sense of smell is estimated to be over 100,000 times greater than ours. Dogs can detect scents over 10 miles away. I remember sitting on a hill with my first dog, Woody, who was old and growing deaf. One day, while we sat there, my partner pulled her car into the driveway over 100 yards away. Woody hadn't seen her arrive, but I could tell he sensed her immediately. He sniffed the air, got up, and trotted across the field to greet her.

So, I look again at my dog lying here peacefully at my feet, sniffing the air and picking up the scents of life all around us. It's hard to fathom what her experience must be like. She smells the chickens next door, the mouse in the grass, the rabbit that was here yesterday. She knows the unique fragrance of every flower, the dandelions, the crabgrass, and the roses. She smells me, the neighbor working in his yard, and each of his dogs playing.

Also, dogs hear more acutely than we do, too. They can hear four times farther and detect higher frequencies. Air vibrations guide them to pinpoint sounds and locations. They can even recognize specific vehicles—like the UPS driver who always brought our dog Honey a treat. She learned the sound of his truck, and even now, years later, whenever she hears a UPS truck, her head perks up in anticipation.

So here I sit with my dog, watching her ears twitch back and forth, picking up distant sounds—a dog barking, birds singing, squirrels chattering, the wind rustling the trees. I whisper her name softly and notice her ears flick as she turns to look at me with those beautiful, trusting eyes. For her, these are the only things that matter. The only things that are real. Her perception of life is so different from ours. I try to imagine her world—to see, smell, and hear as she does. How much am I missing because of my busy mind?

She's just soaking it all in. She isn't wondering how long we'll sit here or what's next. She isn't dwelling on yesterday or worrying about tomorrow. She's content, at peace, connected to the moment and to me.

This is what my dog feels every minute of every day: living in the moment, no past, no future, just now. Basking in life's magic, comforted by love, and blessed by simply being. These observations bring me to a greater understanding of the true meaning of Einstein's words: "Look deep into nature, then you will understand everything better".

Sitting here with my dog, I see the harmony and simplicity of creation, the gift of presence, and the power of love. I feel it awakening new curiosities about how these experiences relate to the greater meaning of life. I feel it is inspiring a meditative journey within me that I believe is leading me to a deeper understanding of love and towards exploration of divine creation.

A journey of... Praying with my dog about love.

CHAPTER
TWO

Love

WHAT IS LOVE?

2 | LOVE

"What is Love?"

T his part of my journey is more about asking questions than getting answers. It's an exploration into the nature of love itself! What if real love is something entirely different than any way I've ever thought of it in the past? I'm starting to feel it's more of a living energy connecting our spirits to the essence of life itself. If so, what might be the implications of that? That would imply all of nature must also be tapped into this energy. Which would mean they experience love as an emotion in ways we do not yet understand. Could we be the ones who are disconnected, possibly hindered by our own limited misconceptions of love? Could love be the very expression of life?

They say God is love. If that's true, are love, life, and God one and the same? And if so, does the eternal nature of God mean that the love we feel—and our living spirits—are eternal as well? The more I focus on this feeling of love within me, the more curious I become about its nature and origin. It seems like something much more than just a thought in my brain or a feeling in my heart. No—it's an emotion, a sense, an energy that feels alive, like a living force within me. And I know it's inside my dog too. That awareness makes me realize it must also exist in other living things. What about all of nature? Is this energy everywhere in ways I can't yet comprehend?

Turning back to my dog lying at my feet, I pet her head, and she presses her ear into my hand before resting her head on my feet. I watch her lying there peacefully and feel a spiritual warmth connecting us.

Curious about how she feels about me, I begin reflecting on the ways she shows her love. I think about how I understand love, how it differs depending on whom I love, and how complex human love can be. I wonder if a dog's love is simpler, yet perhaps deeper and more mysterious. Maybe, in its purest form, love is something nature taps into effortlessly, while we complicate it with our tangled emotions. Perhaps it's our complexity that blinds us to love's true essence.

Expressions of Love

So, why do I think my dog loves me? Before going deeper into the nature of love, I want to step back and think more about the ways my dog shows her love every day— through her actions, instincts, and unique quirks. I'm curious about things like: Does she love me the same way I love her? Why would that warm affection in my heart feel any different for her than it does for me?

She loves to sleep on my bed. Some say it's a sign of affection and a desire to be close, and I believe that. Others argue it's instinctual—dogs seeking warmth and security with their pack. So for me, as the leader of her pack, is this sensation love, or a need for security, or both? And if it's both, does her 'instinct' feel as emotionally fulfilling to her as 'affection' does to me?

She likes to lick my pillow. She'll lie there, licking it almost in a trance. Some suggest it's stress or boredom, while others say it's about the salt or skin cells left behind. There may be some truth in that, but I believe it's more of a comfort behavior tied to affection and our bond. I let her do it because I think it brings her a sense of peace and love.

She kisses me. If I lie down while she's licking my pillow, she'll switch to licking my face—not just a quick lick, but repeated 'kisses'. Then, she'll nestle her head into my neck and lay there peacefully, her head pressed close to mine. In those moments, I can feel her energy, just as she feels mine, and we lie there quietly, love's warmth flowing between us. Sometimes, we even fall asleep like that. It feels like shared love.

We actually 'hold' hands. Often when she wants to shake, she doesn't just give me her paw—I feel the fingers of her paw squeezing my hand. I squeeze back and it feels like holding hands with another person. I've never had another dog do this, so it feels like a unique experience and true moment of spiritual connection.

She carries pieces of me. Many dogs bring toys to play, but she prefers my hat or gloves, carrying them off to lie with. I call it 'taking pieces of me'. Sometimes, she'll even take my hat right off my head or nap with her head resting on it. She likes to sleep with her head on my slippers, and I've woken up to find a hat or sock on the bed, as if she's saying, "I missed you last night". Hilariously, she loves my partner's bra. At bedtime, she eagerly waits for her to take it off, then carries it away to sleep with. So, in the same way we hold to meaningful things that have emotional ties for us, I believe this behavior in her demonstrates she feels love the way we do.

And she always wants in on the hug. Whenever we hug someone, she tries to climb between us, not wanting to be left out. If my partner and I sit close, deep in conversation, she brings us toys or plants herself between us, staring or pawing at us until we acknowledge her. Once she feels included, she settles down nearby, content that our spiritual energies are connected.

Unconditional Love

We like to believe dogs love us no matter what! Their ability to forgive and their constant affection often make us feel they have a greater capacity for 'unconditional love' than we do. They crave our attention and thrive on our approval, and their forgiving nature reinforces our belief in their unconditional love. Seemingly they love us no matter what we do. In reality, it may be their strong emotional bonds and desire to please us that override any negative experiences. In a way, they do love us unconditionally—or at least it feels that way.

But maybe there's even more to what appears as 'unconditional love' than that. What if it's not about love but more of a practical behavioral response? Maybe dogs don't even perceive things like neglect or cruelty the same way we do. In their world, maybe behaviors we consider abuse or mistreatment might not appear to them in the same way. Perhaps what we see as physical punishment appears to them more as a correction from their pack leader. For example, if we forget to feed them, they may not view our neglect as abuse or punishment, but rather as–this is simply a time where there's a scarcity of food and water. More as a natural 'bad time' when resources are low. So instead of taking it personally, they seem to live fully in the moment, happy to be with us until the difficulty passes.

If that's true, perhaps they don't need to forgive in the way we understand forgiveness—because they never frame these experiences as betrayals. Instead, their joy, trust, and loyalty endure, and we interpret that as a purer form of love.

Imagine coming home every day to someone so overjoyed they're practically leaping with excitement. Dogs seem to embody a kind of love that feels like total, unconditional acceptance. Even when we've done something to make them feel bad, they don't hold grudges. They're always happy to see us.

Maybe this is because dogs love differently than we do. They don't seem to attach conditions, expectations, or judgments to their affection. It's simple and pure—more like deep trust and faith than anything else. Their love might be a reflection of something we struggle to achieve, a kind of love that simply exists, no matter what.

So what can we learn from nature about love?

So, what do we really know about love? Sitting here with my dog lying peacefully at my feet, I'm distracted by a bird flying to her nest. I wonder: Wouldn't this feeling of love feel the same for all living things? The bird protects her babies, but does she love them? We know gorillas show emotion and great affection toward their young. Elephants mourn the loss of family for days. Do animals feel love in the same way we do?

And what about plants? They don't have brains or hearts, but they respond to stimuli. Trees, for example, communicate with one another. When one tree is harmed, neighboring trees initiate biological responses to help. Science would argue these are protective behaviors. But could they actually be a form of love we humans don't yet have a capacity to understand?

These thoughts lead me to reflect more deeply on how humans experience love. When I think about love, the first thing that comes to mind for me is that warm, affectionate emotion we associate with the word—that undeniable sense we feel in our hearts. But when I really think about it I realize there are many dimensions to what we mean when we say we love something.

We equate so many different feelings with love. We feel it, we crave it, and we need it to be happy. Without it, we feel empty, sad, and unfulfilled. At younger ages, when we fall in love, more often than not, driven by instinctual desires towards physical attraction we perceive it as 'true' love. And we love our family and friends differently than we love romantic partners. And as we grow older, our love deepens into a greater affection. It's not unusual for people to say they feel more love for their dog than most human relationships? There are so many dimensions to all of these forms of love. So 'love' is an emotion we experience on so many different levels.

Humans make love so complicated. We attach conditions to it. "As long as you are this, I love you. If not, I don't". As if it is something we can turn off and on as if love were less of an emotion and more of a decision. Why are we so unforgiving? Can true love be withheld? How can we love someone and then stop loving them? Did we ever truly love them?

And what about lust? Lust is desire, but does desire equate to love? Consumed by desire, we lose our ability to think straight. When we believe we've fallen in love—found our soulmate—it's as if we've lost our brains, our lover can do no wrong and no one can convince us otherwise. But is it really love, or just desire? And then when the desire fades, we often discover we didn't really know that person at all. Yet, that doesn't mean lust doesn't serve an instinctual purpose. Love, in all its form, does seem to evoke a desire to fulfill itself.

In all of the natural world, sexual desire plays an essential role motivating nature's need to procreate. For animals, mating is about reproduction. The motivation may be driven by a natural sexual desire, but the goal is almost always procreation. Humans, on the other hand, complicate sex. Typically, our first motivation is not about procreation but rather seeking it for pleasure. We attach conditions to it and often use it as a way to prove our love. Animals don't confuse sex with love.

This highlights how much more complex love is for humans. Perhaps it has something to do with how our more

developed brains make us analyze everything more. But that doesn't mean we understand love better. In fact, our complicated brains may drive us toward overindulgences that prevent us from experiencing true love. Maybe we've confused it so much we've lost touch with its essence.

I'm starting to believe the true essence of love is much greater. What if love is a divine, living energy that fuels all life, experienced in countless ways? What if love is the very essence of life itself? Life as a burning flame, and love as the energy that keeps it alive.

The more I meditate on love, the more amazed I am by its power and omnipresence. It feels so real, so alive—I can feel it in every cell of my being. It's a powerful, mysterious force. But what makes it happen? Where does it come from? What if love isn't just an emotion, but a divine energy—the lifeblood of all creation?

Revelations of Love, learned with my dog!

And what does all this have to do with my dog loving me? It adds a deeper, totally new perspective to what her love might be like. It makes me think differently about the relationships I share with her, and with everyone close to me, in terms of how they are so much more special than I ever realized. Like a stream of divine energy that connects us all to all living things.

I'm feeling the stronger the love we feel, the more eternally connected we are on a spiritual level. Like soulmates our souls—our life energies—travel together beyond this version of ourselves. Maybe this is why we feel such strong connections to certain individuals. Perhaps the love we feel is not only an emotion rooted in eternal spiritual bonds but also the energy that fuels life itself.

So yes, I do believe my dog loves me the way I love her. The point is that love is not just a feeling we share. It is a connection between spiritual energies that travel together through the eternal stream of life. We are essential to each other's existence. This connection determines our attraction, our dedication, and our love. We travel together as one, forever.

Sitting here with my dog, meditating or praying on the nature of love, I feel as though all these thoughts are just tiny manifestations of something far greater. Love, I'm beginning to sense, is so much more than anything I've understood before.

I'm beginning to feel 'Love is God'!

The more I meditate on love, the more amazed I am by its power—its omnipresence. There is no doubt of its presence in everything. It feels so real and alive that I can sense it in every cell of my being. I understand how the biological functions and physical sensations of my body work, but the real mystery is this 'feeling', this mysterious emotion or power living inside me? Where does it come from? What brings it to life?

Consider the idea that love is much more than just an emotion. Could love be all there is? What if love is life itself—the fundamental essence of everything? Perhaps 'Love' is a mysterious spiritual energy force that fuels life itself!

But what does that mean? It brings to mind so many more thoughts and questions. Where is this taking me? It makes me feel the need to meditate or pray more deeply about this 'feel-good' emotion I've been trying to understand. I'm really starting to feel 'Love' is something much greater and more powerful than I've ever imagined. Like 'Love' is actually a mysterious power, emotion, or divine spiritual energy that is the living essence of God.

If God is love, and love is the spiritual energy within us, then love is what connects us all to God. This reminds me of the Bible verse (1 John 4:16): *"God is love, and all who live in love live in God, and God lives in them. God is love, and he who abides in love abides in God, and God in him."*

Reflecting back on my earlier musings, I think about how the shared love of my dog has been my entry point into this deeper understanding. Perhaps her way of loving is closer to the essence of divine love than all of my human pondering and analyzing. She's taught me to see love as something far greater than I ever imagined.

This meditation—or prayer—with my dog about love has led me to a whole new understanding of God. And to truly know love, I need to truly know God. In this search for love, I'm realizing that love is far greater and more omnipresent than these simple concepts I've discussed so far. To truly know love, I haven't even begun to ask the right questions. If love is indeed the living essence of God, then we all hold within us a connection to something infinite and divine. What might this mean for how we live, love, and relate to the world around us?

So now, at this point in my journey, I'm feeling led to seek a deeper understanding of God. I've realized I'm only beginning to grasp the depth of love.

Time again to sit and... "Pray with my dog!"

CHAPTER THREE

God

LOVE IS GOD!

3 | GOD

"Love Is God!"

I. DISCOVERING GOD

I'm pretty certain my dog never contemplates God. Watching her lie peacefully in the grass, I ponder what goes on in her mind. I know she's acutely aware of the sounds and scents surrounding her. Unlike me, she's attuned to every little detail without her brain being consumed by the day's plans and problems. She simply absorbs it all, existing in the moment, every minute of every day. The concepts of God, spirit, life's purpose, or eternity never cross her mind. None of that matters to her. There's no need for such questions to even arise, which only deepens my curiosity about her experience.

Focusing on these thoughts, my mind starts to unwind. I become more attuned to my surroundings. I observe the birds singing in the trees, the squirrels darting about, the bees buzzing around the clover, and the ants bustling in the grass. None of them ponder God either. They, like my dog, are just part of the flow of life. They live it without overthinking it, simply going about their roles, contributing their part to the ecosystem, living until they pass away. And even then, they likely don't dwell on death because they understand it's part of the natural cycle.

Albert Einstein once said, *"Look deep into nature, then you will understand everything better."*

In nature's tapestry, none of these creatures consider God, the afterlife, or eternity because such concepts hold no relevance or importance for them. Why is that? Why are we, humans, the only ones preoccupied with these questions? Could it be that they are more naturally connected to God? Do they grasp the essence of life and the divine better than we do?

Is my dog more connected to God than me?

What if animals don't consciously think about God because, for them, being in tune with their instincts means being connected to God? They might not perceive God as a separate, all-powerful deity but rather as a pervasive presence or energy that encompasses everything. For them, understanding their role in life and eternity, and their connection with God, might not be a conscious thought because it's simply the way things are. They don't even think of themselves as dogs, bees as bees, or birds as birds. To them, all living beings are just part of the fabric of existence, each fulfilling its purpose without the need for introspection or comparison with other species.

It's similar to breathing air. You do it without thinking because it's essential to your existence. For animals, life and God are intertwined. This means that every living thing is a manifestation of God. So, they don't ponder about God because, in a sense, they are already part of the divine. The spiritual energy that animates every living being is, in essence, God. If this is true, then I am God, my dog is God, that tree is God, the grass is God, and so on. Anything with living energy is a manifestation of the divine. If living energy is synonymous with God, then we may not be separate living entities but rather part of one massive, eternal life force of spiritual energy, all interconnected and unified in God. This concept suggests that we are all created in the likeness of God, collectively forming one divine entity.

Observing my dog sleeping peacefully, I am struck by the vitality within her, the living energy that defines her existence. This realization extends to myself and all living things, as I become acutely aware of the pulsating life force, this electric energy called life, flowing through me, through her, through us all. I look around and sense it in the birds, bees, squirrels, and even in the grass, flowers, and trees.

This perspective offers a fascinating way to contemplate God. It prompts me to meditate or pray deeply on this concept, to explore where it leads. It raises profound questions about the nature of this 'life energy.' Is it a soul? Is it a spirit? Could it be God?

<u>So, what is this energy? Where does it come from?</u>

Again, as I gaze at my peacefully sleeping dog, I'm struck by her warm, beautiful body, realizing that she exists in this form because of the billions of atoms spinning, connecting, and interacting to give her life and identity. Similarly, I sit here, occupying this space, having these thoughts, feeling this energy pulsing through my body realizing I too am made up of this energy. Contemplating this, I feel a profound sense of connection to all living beings around me, as if this vital energy links us all. Not only to each other but all of nature, the moon, the stars, the galaxies, the eternal power of the universe, uniting us with everything and with God.

Perhaps, in an ethereal way, this energy even opens a shared channel for communication among us. Maybe this has something to do with why, when we look at each other, we just sense how we feel or know what each other is thinking. As if we're able to tap into this energy stream we all share and, especially for those close to us, we connect our thoughts and feelings without even speaking. Maybe this is a communication channel that even explains intuition or feelings we pick up from situations or others we don't even know as well.

At first, this idea worked well for me when considering 'living' things. It was easy to see how this energy could be the life force, akin to our spirit or soul. However, the realization that atoms also make up all 'non-living' things began to complicate my thinking. How could this energy be just a life force if it also exists in rocks?

This realization led me to consider things in a more expansive manner. If everything, living and nonliving, is made up of atoms with active energy, how can we differentiate between living and nonliving? I understand the distinction that living things have cellular organisms while non-living things do not. To those of you with scientific backgrounds, I acknowledge that my observations are uneducated and, at best, rudimentary. Nevertheless, the fact remains that atomic energy exists in non-living matter, prompts the question: what is this energy that essentially never dies? Since this atomic energy exists in both living and nonliving things, how does that affect my notion that this force might be the manifestation of God? What about non-living things? Does this mean we are similarly connected to rocks? Are rocks also God?

This puts a very different spin on how I think about all this. If I stop thinking of things as living vs. nonliving, and start thinking of everything as either Spiritual or Material, I begin to get a whole different perspective on creation.

First I need to ask myself, "What is Matter, or the Material?"

Science tells us, all material creation, whether living or nonliving, is made up of matter composed of atoms. Atoms are the fundamental building blocks of everything, including humans, animals, plants, rocks, dirt, air, and water, and these atoms are eternal and indestructible. They consist of a nucleus containing elements or chemical compounds that make up the 'matter,' as well as electrons that orbit the nucleus, driven by electrical energy. This means that everything, even a rock, possesses energy.

While the nucleus and elemental compounds of atoms represent the visible, touchable, tangible aspects of matter, my curiosity is piqued by the mysterious, invisible, electrical energy or force present in every atom. This energy, which seemingly cannot be destroyed, pervades everything both living and nonliving. But where does it originate?

Observing my peacefully snoozing dog, I can actually feel this energy radiating through every cell in her body. I also feel it within myself and all around me. It's as if we are all connected to a vast, eternal stream of energy, transcending individuality. This energy stream feels almost like a universal spiritual river or a singular cosmic force, uniting us all. In this state, there is no distinction between me and you; we are all part of the same whole.

Could this be what we call God? Is this massive, mysterious energy force the eternal spirit that permeates everything? Could this be what unites us with God, reflecting the image of God? If so, then everything, by extension, would be God.

In a way, we are totally reincarnated every few years!

Scientists explain that, apart from specific areas like parts of our heart, eyes, and brain, every cell in our body regenerates and completely replaces itself multiple times during our lives. This means that most of who I am changes entirely every few years. My hands, bones, blood, skin, hair, face, and more are constantly being renewed, creating entirely new versions of myself. The hands I see as I write this are entirely different from the hands I had just a few years ago. The 'material' parts of me, like the ones everyone recognizes, are constantly disappearing and evolving into new forms. Essentially, the person you hugged a decade ago has vanished, replaced by a completely new me. The me you embrace today is a person you've never touched before.

In a way, our bodies resemble the leaves of a tree, sprouting anew each spring, transforming into vibrant hues in the fall, and then regenerating again in the spring. It's intriguing how this process occurs in every organism within us, except for certain parts of the heart, eyes, and brain, which remain unchanged until we pass away. It's akin to how a tree's leaves constantly change while the trunk and roots endure for the tree's lifetime. While scientists likely have concrete explanations for these phenomena, I sense there's a deeper, more mystical aspect to it all. Is all matter just infinite physical manifestations of God?

So, now let's think about the 'Spiritual'.

Think about it, this mysterious energy is everywhere, right? It's in every atom, and since atoms can't be destroyed, that would also mean this energy is eternal. So, if this mysterious, invisible energy is both everywhere and eternal, could it be a glimpse into what we call God?

As I thought about this I wanted to know more about the physical nature of this energy force. I was curious about atoms, and how much of each atom was composed of matter (the nucleus and electrons) vs. how much of it contained that mystical energy force that binds the electrons to the nucleus. The reason I wanted to look into this is because, as I looked at everything around me, my hands, my dog, and all of nature, it seemed to me that it was the physical 'matter' or atomic particles that made up the majority of everything. In other words, because it's what I could visibly see, I assumed it was the matter that comprised the majority of space in every atom. I was astounded to learn the opposite is true. It's the energy force that comprises the vast majority of what makes up every atom. To put it in perspective, if an atom were the size of a football stadium the nucleus (or matter) part of it would be the size of a marble! The entire rest of the atom consists of the electromagnetic force that binds the electrons which are spinning around the nucleus. That invisible, magical, mysterious energy force is, by many thousands of times, much greater than any part of the mass of every atom.

Think about this! Everything we see and touch, even though it looks like a solid mass, is actually composed of mostly empty space! At an atomic level, most of what we are, is a bunch of floating particles with mostly empty space. This is a little hard to get your head around but, in a way, most of who we are is invisible! And so is everything else we can see! If we were able to see the world at an atomic level, everything we could see, including us, would appear like hives of bees buzzing around in different forms! Another way to visualize this might be to think of a pointillism painting of dots forming three dimensional shapes and images of me, my dog, the trees, buildings and everything. We would even be able to see through everything. The entire universe!

And what about the universe? To fully grasp even a rudimentary view of how massive creation is, as you think about the makeup of everything at an atomic level, also think about how vast the universe really is. To put that in perspective, science tells us... there are more stars in the visible universe than grains of sand on the earth, and just as many molecules in four drops of water! Let that sink in for a minute! It's easy for us to look at the stars and imagine how awesome the universe is. But just think about how small, small really is! If there are that many molecules in

four drops of water, just try to imagine how many molecules must be in each one of us. And then how many molecules exist in the universe! And think about all of those atoms in those molecules that contain the magical, mysterious, eternal energy that binds all of existence together! These are numbers we can't even comprehend! Small is infinitely tiny on a divine scale beyond our imagination!

It's mind boggling to think about all of this! It invites me to rethink the very nature of existence! And the implications of how much empty space and energy exist in everything is astounding! The power of this invisible, magical, mysterious energy is the living energy that binds all of creation. Without this energy, nothing would exist! I feel there are no other words to describe it other than to say, it must be God!

Is everything alive?

The nature of this energy leads me to think deeply about living vs. non-living things. Could this energy actually be a living spirit? Is it more accurate to consider creation in the context of spiritual vs. material?

Science differentiates living from non-living things based on characteristics like cellular organization, metabolism, growth, reproduction, response to stimuli, and genetic material. Living organisms meet these criteria, while non-living things do not. But I'm not sure 'living vs nonliving' are the right categories. Maybe something like 'cellular vs non cellular' might be more scientifically accurate. From a philosophical, or theological, perspective 'spiritual vs. material' would be a better way to think about creation.

Since this all-encompassing energy is the fundamental force that binds all atomic particles, maybe it's actually something much greater than just an 'electrical energy' as science describes it. Maybe this energy that exists in all atoms is actually a living energy! Think of it as a living, mysterious, energy force that permeates everything that fuels life.

That being the case, since this eternal energy exists in everything, even in a rock, it would be reasonable to conclude everything is alive. Just existing or manifesting in different states of being. Me, my dog, all of nature, even rocks, air, water, and even buildings, cars, the entire universe - everything is alive. The only thing that sets us apart is our molecular structures.

At first, this was difficult for me to get my head around. Especially the 'buildings / cars' part! But think about the bigger picture discussed earlier about everything that exists being a bunch of 'floating atomic particles'. So, from that perspective, if we realize they are not 'buildings / cars', but instead like us, my dog, rocks and trees, they are just different manifestations of atomic particles. Most of which contain the exact same atomic particles included in us. If we stop thinking of matter, including us, as distinct things but instead think of all of creation as unique manifestations of matter all making unique contributions to existence and all fueled by this energy life force we start to imagine the mind boggling, massive connectedness of creation.

So if everything is connected, how are we unique?

First I need to understand the 'nature' of this energy. What is it? Where does it come from? What does it feel like? How do I describe it? Scientifically I know it exists, but what's really making me believe it is a 'living' energy?

Atomic particles and the mysterious energy that binds them together explain how matter manifests itself. But that doesn't account for things like emotions, conscious thought and memories. These are all magical, mystical, invisible, and alive energies we know are real because we feel them in our soul. Where do these feelings come from? Our heart, our brain? No, they seem to be coming from somewhere much deeper and more mysterious. They are an energy inside me. They seem to come from nowhere but yet they are everything that is me! They don't come from the matter that makes up the physical me. They are a living energy inside me! Could these feelings be coming from that mysterious energy binding the atoms of my physical body together? Is this my Spirit, or my Soul? Is it God living in me?

Our spirits manifest in emotions, awareness, memories, and drive!

I feel a 'warmth in my heart' as I watch my dog lying peacefully at my feet. Observing her steady breathing, I can't help but think about the mysterious 'energy' that flows through her body, sustaining her life. That same energy flows through me, giving me life as well. But when I reflect on this warm sensation of love in my heart, it becomes clear that this feeling is more than just the result of electrical impulses within atoms. It feels deeper—more profound, mysterious, alive.

This 'energy' feels like something far beyond mere electricity. It's a tangible, living 'feeling' originating from my heart. But how can a 'feeling'—an emotion—be produced by electrical energy? This is an incredibly mysterious process! Where do 'emotions' even come from? I know they're real because I feel them coursing through my body. What is their true source?

If the 'energy' I've been contemplating is a manifestation of my spirit, I'm starting to believe that this 'energy'—my spirit—might also be directly connected to God. So, if 'energy' and 'emotions' are one and the same, wouldn't it follow that this feeling of love is a manifestation of the 'Spirit,' my 'Soul,' or perhaps even God? Maybe, as Christians would say, it is the 'Holy Spirit' itself at work.

As I contemplate this, I wonder about my dog. Does she feel love in the same way I do? Her looks, her wagging tail, and her calm presence by my side suggest that she does. Scientific studies confirm that dogs experience similar emotions, with neuroimaging showing that when dogs interact with their owners, the reward centers in their brains light up, just as they do in humans. This deepens my belief that the energy we feel, known as Love, is not just a human experience but something shared across beings, connecting us on a spiritual level. And if we share this energy, this love, perhaps we all share a Soul.

So, if this mysterious energy we call Love is indeed an emotion that stems from the Spirit, or Soul, and if both I and someone else can feel it, then it stands to reason that we both possess a Soul. But if all matter is composed of atomic structures infused with this same mysterious, electrical energy, why wouldn't everything in the rest of God's creation, in its own way—even in ways beyond our current understanding—experience feelings as well?

And if that's the case, wouldn't it logically follow that all things have a 'Soul'? If the 'Soul' is a manifestation of 'God,' then, like me, wouldn't all things also be expressions of God? It would be as if God is revealing Himself through an infinite variety of forms, each a channel for divine presence across all of creation.

Many other thoughts arise tied to the idea that our spirit and emotions are stored in the energy contained in the atoms of our physical bodies!

Consciousness – What about conscious thought and self-awareness? The ability to think, reason, make decisions,

create, and recognize oneself as a distinct individual—
independent of others—is not something unique to
humans. My dog, for instance, knows the time of day,
understands the subtle signals in every move I make,
and knows exactly when it's time to eat, take a walk, or
play. Even plants exhibit forms of awareness. We know
that trees communicate through their root systems via a
network of fungi, acting as individuals while
simultaneously interacting as part of a larger ecosystem
that works together to protect the forest as a whole.

Some researchers even suggest that basic organisms may
exhibit a rudimentary form of self-awareness, such as
the ability to differentiate between 'self' and 'non-self,' a
vital survival mechanism. Where does this awareness
come from? It must originate from that mysterious energy
that exists within everything. It feels as though consciousness is
intertwined with the energy of my spirit or soul.

Because humans possess unique capabilities in this regard, we
often assume we are the most gifted or superior species.
But are we really? Could consciousness be stored in the
energy of our spirits, shared across all living things, just
expressed in different ways?

Knowledge – As humans, we tend to think we're special
because we build communities, invent technologies, and
create cars, planes, and cities. Yet, in the grand scope of

the universe, we are no more than a microscopic blip, and in terms of all creation, we know virtually nothing. The cosmos, with its billions of stars and galaxies stretching across trillions of miles, has been expanding and evolving since time began and will continue to do so long after eternity. Our tiny blue planet has existed for less than the blink of an eye in comparison, and for billions of years before humans emerged a mere 300,000 years ago.

To put this into perspective, if the entire history of Earth were compressed into a single 24-hour day, humans would only appear in the last few seconds before midnight. Certain types of bacteria appeared around 2.4 billion years ago—making them roughly 8,000 times older than humans—and they are considered to be the oldest living species on the planet today.

The other day, I sat beside a pond watching a frog resting on a lily pad. For hours, it sat there, perfectly still, with no apparent urgency, no schedule to keep. It seemed content to simply exist in the moment, and I imagined it might remain in that state for the entire day. Frogs have been around for over 250 million years, which means they've existed approximately 1,000 times longer than humans. What does he know that we don't know?

What must be going on inside the consciousness of creatures like this frog? What thoughts or experiences might fill their minds as they sit there, day after day? What knowledge might they possess that we, with all our inventions and technologies, have yet to understand?

Could it be that knowledge, like memory and awareness, is stored in the energy of our spirits?

Senses – It's clear that many species possess sensory abilities far beyond our own. For instance, a dog's sense of smell is about 100,000 times more acute than ours. While we might catch the general aroma of vegetable soup simmering on the stove, dogs can discern the individual scents of the carrots, peas, and celery within it. Other species perceive the world in ways we cannot even fathom. Bees, for example, see ultraviolet light patterns on flowers, which guide them to nectar, and certain birds rely on ultraviolet reflections to identify potential mates.

Moreover, many migratory species, such as birds, sea turtles, and some insects, use Earth's magnetic field to navigate across vast distances. Our understanding of reality is confined by the limits of our sensory organs, while the rest of nature experiences sights, sounds, and smells that remain invisible to us. In essence, the world looks, smells, and feels vastly different through the eyes and sensory perceptions of the countless species we share it with.

Could these heightened sensory experiences also be tied to bioelectric patterns? If so, do they carry forward with the energy of the spirit, preserved beyond physical existence? Could our unique sensory perceptions be stored in the energy of our spirits?

Memories – Where do our memories come from, and where are they truly stored? Elephants, like us, have been observed mourning their dead, often revisiting the bones or burial sites of their fallen herd members. Some researchers believe this behavior suggests that elephants hold deep memories of family members who have passed, possibly even connecting them to past generations.

Recent studies on flatworms, particularly planarians, have uncovered intriguing insights into memory storage that challenge traditional views. Scientists have found that planarians retain memories even after their brains are removed and regenerated, suggesting that memory may not solely reside in the brain but could be distributed throughout the body. This discovery points to the idea that memory might be tied to bioelectric patterns interacting with cellular structures, rather than being confined to the brain. It's as though the brain has evolved to store immediately relevant information (similar to a computer's RAM), while deeper memory is embedded in bioelectric cells.

Imagine the implications! Since energy is eternal and never dies, if our memories are stored in bioelectric patterns, it seems logical that our memories, too, are eternal. Could our memories travel with us through time? Are they preserved in the energy of our spirits, carried forward even after physical death?

Talents – Could this explain why we possess unique talents or feel deeper connections with some people more than others? Perhaps our relationships transcend this lifetime, continuing with us forever. Maybe our energies are intertwined, which might help explain the feeling of being soulmates, or of sharing one spirit across infinite experiences. Could this also be why we are born with particular interests, talents, or inclinations?

How often do we witness child prodigies performing at genius levels—playing instruments, painting, or solving complex mathematical problems—prompting us to wonder if they possess the spirits of past masters? Maybe they really do! Why are some of us drawn to art, science, business, or philosophy, while others are not? Perhaps we too are carrying the talents, interests, and memories of past experiences. Are our talents stored within the energy of our spirits, guiding our passions and abilities?

One Spirit, Many Manifestations

We know these powers—self-awareness, conscious thought, and memory—are undeniably real. And it's clear they aren't exclusive to humans. More and more, I'm sensing that these abilities might originate from a divine source.

Could this be the soul? What if this magical, mysterious, invisible energy is actually the eternal stream of God, permeating every part of the universe? Me, you, my dog, the birds, the bees, the grass, rivers, the air we breathe, the moon, the stars—everything, both living and nonliving. All interconnected as one eternal being, unified with nature, and one in God.

Is everything part of one spirit? If this energy manifests as emotions, awareness, and conscious thought, wouldn't it suggest that all of existence, in some form, is experiencing a level of awareness? Perhaps our current understanding of awareness is too limited, unable to grasp its full extent. Given that this atomic energy permeates all things, could it be that the source of all existence is one eternal soul or spirit? Not a collection of individual souls separated from God, but a single Great Spirit expressing itself in infinite physical manifestations throughout creation. Could this be what is meant by being "created in the image of God"? And is this what Jesus meant when he said, "The Kingdom of God is within you" (Luke 17:21)?

Many Manifestations, each with their own purpose!

Many more questions come to mind. If this idea of one spirit in all things is true, how can we be separate, unique individuals? Am I still "me"? Why do we all have different ideas, behaviors, goals, dreams, and beliefs? If all existence is united by one spirit, why does that spirit need to manifest in so many diverse forms? Why are there humans, dogs, trees, suns, stars, and galaxies? Why does God allow for positive and negative energies or the need to procreate? If this is all true, why would God choose such complexity? Why not simply eliminate all matter and exist as one happy, eternal spirit, without the need for all these material manifestations? Maybe this complexity is just how God operates.

How can we be both unique individuals and part of one spirit at the same time? We know all existence is composed of matter, which evolves, lives, and dies in various ways. Evolution is the mechanism of the universe. If God is the great creator of the universe and utilizes evolution to manifest creation, then God must, in some sense, be evolution. But does God guide evolution through design and intention, or is God a conscious energy with dreams of creation, allowing it to evolve freely? Perhaps each of us, and all of nature, are unique physical manifestations of God, each with our own purpose, driven by the shared spirit of God's creative impulse. In this sense, everything in existence shares the one spirit of God, yet we each have a unique role in the grand tapestry of the natural order.

If we accept that consciousness, awareness, memory, and emotion are all manifestations of the same divine energy, it leads to the idea that everything in the universe is connected. Could it be that this energy is the eternal stream of God flowing through all creation? If so, then we are all one with each other, one with nature, and one with God. One divine energy of God residing within all of us, manifesting in different forms.

II. EXPLORING GOD

So, if this Spirit within us is God, why do we feel the need to create or accomplish things? In other words, if God is the creator of everything, and if we are God already within us, why would we feel any desire to *be* something? Why would we need to achieve anything at all? Wouldn't everything already be perfect? Well, maybe it's because the very essence of God is creation, and God expresses this through us, using us as instruments to experience life. God, after all, loves to create, to expand, to grow, to evolve. And so, as vessels of God, we have God's desire to achieve, to create within us. We are God evolving—endlessly manifesting Creation. This might explain why each of us is imbued with unique talents, goals, desires, and dreams. We are the tools through which God grows infinite possibilities.

But, while that sounds nice, it raises a question: if God is the perfect creator, and we are God's instruments of manifestation, wouldn't that imply everything we do should turn out perfect? And yet, we know that's not the case! Unless...we recognize that Creation isn't about perfection—it's about evolution. Perhaps God is more about the process of evolving than with creating something perfect. Maybe the true measure of success in Creation isn't achieving a final, predetermined result.

Consider this: a painting imagined in the dreams of an artist can only become real when the artist picks up a brush and applies paint to canvas. Without the paint and canvas, that painting remains an unfulfilled dream. We are the paint and brushes in God's eternal painting. As the saying goes, "life's about the journey, not the destination." Creation, like life, is an ongoing journey, not a completed masterpiece

God likes to feel and do things!

Maybe the simple answer is that God loves to feel good and to touch and experience things. God is much more than spirit—God is everything, including matter. God wants to see, smell, taste, and create, so God's spiritual energy manifests into physical matter, like us, for that very purpose. All material things, including me, my dog, and all of creation, are simply instances of God's experience, coming and going throughout eternity. Perhaps we, and everything around us, are living manifestations of God's eternal dreams. We are God dreaming of touching, feeling, laughing, crying, creating, and evolving. God is the music, and we, along with all of creation, are the instruments. Each of us has a unique, individual role in fulfilling God's imagination.

And yes, while all of creation is one in spirit with God, we are also real and unique individuals. God loves beauty, so we create art, music, and poetry. God loves to feel love, so we kiss, hug, and hold one another. God loves creation, so we invent things. God loves harmony, so we share our lives with family, friends, and community. God loves diversity, so we each have unique talents and interests. But God's creation far exceeds our human experiences. God loves nature, so there are plants and animals. God loves infinity, so there are stars, galaxies, and a universe without beginning or end. God loves eternity, so creation evolves forever and never dies. God even loves to communicate with us, which is why we have angelic messengers—like my dog!

And it's not just us. God creates different species because they, too, possess abilities that contribute to God's masterpiece in ways we humans don't even understand. We often think that only humans, or other living things, matter to God. But it's not just living things. We forget that non-living things also play essential roles in Creation, providing the foundations upon which life depends for survival and existence. We often overlook the fact that the molecular matter that makes us is not so different from the molecular makeup of the earth, air, and water. Life cannot exist without non-life, and both living and nonliving matter share that mysterious energy force binding everything at the subatomic level.

So instead of categorizing things as either living or nonliving, perhaps a better understanding of Creation is to see everything as a blend of atomic matter and spiritual energy. In this sense, all species—including what we perceive as non-living things—are tools of God, contributing to the growth and evolution of Creation in ways humans cannot provide or comprehend. All of us, all matter, all of existence, are simply infinite expressions, lenses, or paths for God to expand and create. This might be what makes us both unique individuals and one with God at the same time.

<u>Orderly processes preserve free evolution!</u>

Does God need rules? If we all share the same spirit of God, why are some of us natural leaders while others are followers?

We know that there is a natural order—a set of rules by which everything depends for its existence. In nature, bees rely on a queen to build honeycombs and make honey. Dogs need leaders to help the pack work together for survival. Parents must provide for their families through work. Communities establish laws so that they can function harmoniously. Nature needs the rhythm of the seasons to renew the cycle of life. The universe operates under physical laws—gravity that keeps planets in orbit, molecular and atomic dependencies that prevent the cosmos from spinning chaotically into oblivion.

But are these laws consciously created and planned by God? Or are they the natural, evolutionary result of God's spiritual energy in the ongoing process of creation? Does God set these laws deliberately, or do they emerge naturally from the essence of the divine presence that permeates all of creation?

Perhaps it doesn't really matter how or why these laws exist—what matters is that they do. The spiritual energy of God could manifest itself through an evolutionary process, where the organization of life, nature, and the universe emerges from that same divine essence, allowing for both order and chaos, structure and freedom.

We see this interplay between rules and freedom in everything around us. From the way societies form laws to maintain order, to the instinctual rules that govern animal behavior, all the way down to the molecular rules that hold matter together. It's as if creation itself is both following and evolving through the spiritual energy of God, expressing a delicate balance between order and chaos—a balance that allows life, nature, and the universe to thrive.

In the end, what seems clear is that whether these laws are consciously made by God or naturally evolving through the divine essence, they provide the framework that allows creation to exist and evolve. Just as a community needs laws to thrive, the universe seems to require some kind of order, an inherent set of rules that flow naturally from the energy that sustains it all.

<u>So what if there is no grand plan?</u>

What if it's orderly chaos, with God simply flowing? Maybe God is less of a being who thinks and plans, and more of an omnipresence that evolves—an existence that just *is*. But if that's the case, does God still have a conscious purpose?

When I meditate or pray on these thoughts, I feel unsettled. These questions aren't what I expected or wanted, but they resonate with me. And as I continue meditating, I become more comfortable with them. The idea builds: perhaps God isn't an entity controlling every outcome or shaping everything according to a master plan. Instead, God could be a spiritual energy permeating everything with an instinctual drive to create consciously. Creation itself involves experimentation and free expression—it suggests controlled chaos, which isn't a bad thing. I know this because I function similarly. I have ideas, I make plans, I use orderly processes to create, but I don't control every outcome. So, I can relate to how this orderly chaos might work for God. I make mistakes, things don't always go as expected, and I end up trying again or being led to something new. Maybe that's how it is for God too—letting the universe interact and adjust the outcomes through evolutionary processes. This would mean that God is continually experimenting, allowing creation to evolve and manifest the limitless possibilities in God's imagination.

And what about dreams?

Does this imply that what we imagine in dreams could be real? If we consider dreams in this context, then yes, they could absolutely be real—just as real as our experiences when awake. Maybe dreams are moments where our physical bodies rest, but our spirits are freed from the boundaries of what we perceive as reality. These moments allow our spirits to reconnect with eternity on a parallel level while our bodies materialize experiences that, in the grand scheme, last for less than the blink of an eye. So, as our spirits travel through dreams, experiencing connections with other people, places, and things, perhaps these experiences are just as real as our waking life, only on a different plane or dimension. In this way, dreams could be just as tangible as our conscious reality, serving as a means—like prayer—to connect with the eternal spirit. It's a dimension where all spirits converge, whether living or dead, across past, present, and future. In dreams, we can fly, be in many places at once, visit loved ones, relive memories, walk on water, pass through walls, and reunite with my dogs. I've even dreamt of being both male and female at the same time, talking to squirrels, leaping between buildings. As strange as these experiences sound, in my dreams they all seem perfectly normal and make sense. So maybe dreams aren't just wild fantasies—maybe they're times when our bodies rest while our spirits play freely in a parallel dimension that's just as real as our waking world.

Many traditions believe our soul exists beyond our current reality.

There are esoteric traditions and schools of thought that question whether anything is truly real. What if our reality is nothing more than a dream in the mind of God? Physicists entertain the idea of parallel dimensions or universes, and some even wonder whether our spirits play out the same experiences on multiple planes of existence simultaneously. Could our souls exist beyond the limitations of our current perception of reality?

If we accept the idea that the spirit, or soul, is the one spirit of God manifesting through different bodies to experience creation in various ways, then it seems reasonable to consider that our spirits could also be playing out experiences on other planes of existence at the same time. If this is happening here, why wouldn't it be happening elsewhere—perhaps in the many dreams of God? Maybe our dreams aren't just figments of our imagination, but glimpses into experiences in parallel dimensions.

As wild as this may sound, many traditions and philosophies propose similar ideas. I've always been drawn to the Hawaiian concept of Ho'oponopono and the idea of 'aka chords'—spiritual threads that bind us to everything, used in rituals of healing and reconciliation. Plato's allegory of the cave suggests that the world we perceive is merely shadows on a wall, with true reality existing beyond our sensory experiences. In Hindu philosophy, *Maya* refers to the illusion of the physical world, which hides the ultimate reality. In modern physics, Multiverse Theory posits that infinite universes might exist parallel to our own, each presenting different variations of reality. String Theory suggests the existence of multiple dimensions beyond the familiar three dimensions of space and one of time.

Hinduism and Buddhism also speak of the soul's journey through different planes of existence, including various levels of consciousness or realms of reincarnation. Esoteric Christianity considers the soul eternal, moving through multiple lifetimes and planes as part of its spiritual journey. Panentheism proposes that God is greater than the universe and includes it, while still transcending it. Non-dualism argues that there is no true separation between the self and the universe—all is one, with separations being mere illusions. Shamanic practices often include journeys to alternate realities, where people experience vivid, impactful encounters. Some Quantum Consciousness Theories even speculate that consciousness itself could be a fundamental aspect of the universe, perhaps linking different dimensions or realities.

<u>So, is anything real, or is it all in my imagination?</u>

I say yes—everything is real! All of these experiences are manifesting in physical reality. Think of the mysterious energy force that binds atomic particles into molecules as the spirit of God, using me and all of creation to physically manifest the sensations of evolving creation. My hands type these words, which others are able to read. I paint and share my art, music inspires me to dance, and I enjoy coffee in the morning. I am filled with awe at nature: majestic mountains, stars in the night sky, rushing streams, ocean waves, and the gentle feeling of the wind on my skin. I feel love in a kiss, comfort in a hug, joy in holding my soulmate's hand. I experience the unconditional devotion of my dog, and I am thankful for every blessing, achievement, and adventure life brings me. These sensations are real because I experience them with all my senses.

But even if these experiences occur in this reality or in our dreams—or perhaps in other dimensions—does it matter whether or not they are "real" in the traditional sense? If we are conscious of them, then they are real, regardless of how or where we experience them.

III. QUESTIONING GOD

So far, this exploration has been inspiring and enlightening, but then something occurred to me that complicated the picture significantly. If God is all-powerful and omnipresent, the creator of all things, why is there pain, suffering, failure, or evil? If nothing happens outside of God's plan, why allow these negative experiences at all? If you control everything, why spoil the beauty with hardship? Is this part of a cosmic joke, or does it hint that perhaps God doesn't have complete power over all things?

What are these contradictions all about?

At first, these thoughts troubled me deeply, making me question everything. If God isn't perfect, could that mean God makes mistakes, isn't in control, or, worse, harbors evil? This internal conflict was unsettling. But after meditating on it, a new concept began to form, one that started to make sense of it all.

I began thinking about that mystical positive / negative energy contained in all atoms that's required for all creation to exist. And then I started thinking about myself and how I rely on contradictions every day. Sometimes I succeed, sometimes I fail, sometimes I'm kind, and sometimes I'm selfish. None of these contradictions alone define me but I need all of them to fully understand any of them. If I never knew hunger I wouldn't fully appreciate having food. When I fail at something it drives me to keep trying until I succeed.

The same holds true for emotions. Good needs bad to be appreciated; happiness needs sadness to be recognized. Without contrast, 'good' or 'happy' would just be the constant state of things and would lose all meaning. This extends to all aspects of life: there is no spring without winter, no life without death, no warmth without cold. Without darkness, how could we appreciate light?

Thomas Edison famously said, "I have not failed 10,000 times—I've successfully found 10,000 ways that will not work." Without failure he would not have invented the light bulb. Success requires failure. So, contradictions are necessary. The trick is to find balance between the extremes.

<u>In this way, Life is more about 'balance' than contradictions!</u>

This balance between opposites is mirrored in nature, even down to the atomic level, where positive and negative charges hold matter together. Life and death, positive and negative forces—these are the principles that make everything possible. God, then, isn't imperfect, evil, or out of control. Rather, God is the infinite, balanced energy that fuels this creative evolution, where opposites are necessary for creation to exist. In other words, God is everything, spiritual and material, and God requires balance for creation to evolve. Whenever one side outweighs the other, (energy vs. matter) corrections are necessary to bring the extremes back into harmonious balance. Positive and negative aren't just forces in our lives; they're the very building blocks of the universe itself.

So how does all of this relate to divine justice and fairness?

But it's still troubling to see how unfair these opposites can be. Why do some people suffer immensely while others get to live charmed lives? On a philosophical level, an explanation might be, misfortune generates compassion thereby encouraging human kindness and generosity. On a microbiological level, the very same microbe that causes disease in one person may be essential to saving the life of another. What seems bad in one context might be good in another. The existence of contradictions doesn't always feel fair, and depending on the circumstances can seem to be either good or bad.

But on a practical level, why did God pick me? Why do I have to suffer? Perhaps the easiest way to relate to this is to think about baby sea turtles. Thousands hatch in the sand at the same time and begin a mass race to the water. Some make it but most get taken by seagulls in their attempt to make it to the water. Those that make it will carry on the next generation of turtles. Those that don't make it contribute to the next generation of seagulls. God doesn't choose which turtle makes it and which one doesn't. But in God's balance of creation enough sea turtles make it to continue sea turtles and enough do not to continue seagulls. God consciously loves both the sea turtles and the seagulls and uses evolutionary creation to sustain them both.

<u>With that in mind, how does that relate to me?!</u>

I've worked pretty hard all my life and have to live on a pretty tight budget. Yet, I have good friends who never had a job, inherited a lot of money and can do anything they want. Why do they get to live a charmed life and I have to struggle to pay my bills? But as I think of that on a deeper level I realize I have a roof over my head, food in my refrigerator, live in a peaceful community and have family, friends and a dog that loves me! That puts me in the top 20% of the wealthiest people on the planet! And not only that, I learn other things about my 'charmed life' friends. One of them seems pretty balanced and happy with life. But another is now a drug addict and fights depression because they were given so much, they never found purpose and turned to drugs. Still another, got wrapped up in the pleasures of wealth but lost touch with their kids, ended in terrible divorce, and struggles with loneliness.

But if we are all God, why aren't we all born with the same opportunities?

My mother ended up totally crippled by Multiple Sclerosis and died at an early age. If God is in her, just like God is in me, why would God choose to manifest in that existence? Although the answer might seem unsettling, like the sea turtles, God didn't choose! Because God is about Creation, and God uses evolution to manifest material existence, and evolution by definition does not always manifest exactly the same way each time. This leaves the possibility for things like genetic disorders to occur. So does this mean God is not in control? Maybe God uses random outcomes because that's the real beauty of evolutionary creation? But God always uses a balance of positives and negatives in creation. So in that way, God is always in control. For example, in the case of MS, it is known to inspire personal growth. It can foster resilience, patience, and a deeper appreciation for life. The challenges it brings can sometimes push individuals and their loved ones to reflect on what truly matters. Scientifically, MS has led to innovations in medical treatments, including the development of disease-modifying therapies and better diagnostic tools. The pursuit of finding a cure for MS contributes to our broader understanding of human biology and can drive breakthroughs in other fields of medicine.

Some say, God has a plan for everything and it's not for me to question God's 'plan'. I've always had a problem with that because if nothing happens that's not in God's plan, why pray for anything, or why not just do anything I want. If God doesn't want it to happen, it won't happen. If God wants it to happen, it's going to happen regardless of what I want. It implies I have no responsibility or control over anything. This is troublesome because it suggests we should just accept it when God makes, what appear to be,'unjust' decisions.

Is it divine justice, or balanced evolution?

Some traditions like Buddhism and Hinduism view adversity as a result of past actions (karma), but also as a means to cultivate virtues like patience, resilience, and compassion. Others even believe we exist simultaneously in different dimensions and we experience events differently in each at the same time. In these ways, we can envision possibilities where, in multiple incarnations, we experience many different conditions of the same events. While these concepts may be difficult to get your head around it really doesn't matter whether they have any relevance to specific ways of believing. The point is most traditions recognize and present ideas for resolution of apparent unjust contradictions in life.

As it relates to this meditation, I'm more comfortable with the idea that God requires positive / negative influences for balanced evolution of creation and we are God's tool for resolving contradictions.

It plays out the same way in all of the natural world. Like the sea turtles, sometimes one is just luckier than the other. The strong overcome the weak to ensure healthy procreation of species. The vulnerable provide sustenance for the survival of others. Seasonal changes preserve our natural world through cycles of life and death.

We don't have to wonder if this is right. God is on display right before our eyes. God is revealed in positive and negative influences in everything that exists.

So God didn't pick on me!

God IS me manifesting in one tiny experience of creation. The idea that God uses balance to resolve contradictions seems to provide a more relatable way to think about God's influence over outcomes. God is a balance of positives and negatives eternally playing out in infinite physical, emotional and spiritual ways.

So God consciously dreams a vision and uses positive and negative influences to evolve creation. God plays this out using me to plant flowers and provide water for their growth while I wait with anticipation to experience the beauty of their blooms. And then God uses me to experience the smell of their fragrance and see their beauty with my eyes. This is how God thrills at experiencing the unexpected beauty of creation as it manifests. In this way, God uses free will and random outcomes to contribute to the process. But the final result is always subject to a balance of contradictions. God provides the conscious intent that assures all possibilities play by the rules of balance to ensure preservation of the natural order!

<u>We are one in God experiencing creation in an infinite number of ways!</u>

The awesome beauty of Creation, by its nature, is unpredictable, evolving through both positive and negative experiences. God, it seems, consciously utilizes this randomness as part of the process of creation, where positive and negative results are both needed. The key is to remember that everything is part of this larger cycle, and we are all manifestations of God playing out different roles in eternal creation. Every experience, whether we perceive it as good or bad, is fleeting in the grand scheme of things. We, as parts of God, evolve and manifest in infinite ways, perhaps even experiencing multiple realities and dimensions simultaneously. Across different incarnations, we all experience both success and failure.

This understanding helps me see that contradictions aren't signs of imperfection, but rather necessities for evolution. God doesn't choose one path or one person over another; each of us is a unique manifestation of the same divine energy. Our individual experiences—whether human, animal, or nature—are all part of this greater whole. We are all one in God, experiencing creation in countless, infinite ways.

<u>Your spirit is God in you and everything around you!</u>

I need to pause for a moment and look at my dog lying at my feet. As I hold her and pet her soft fur, I gaze into her eyes, and I recognize the same energy, the same spirit of God flowing through both of us. Hugging her, I feel love radiating between us, as if we are two manifestations of one soul. At the same time, I'm struck by the wonder and blessing of experiencing these unique physical forms that express our shared spirit.

You can try this yourself. Step outside and stop thinking about the constant swirl in your mind. Listen to the sounds of nature—birds chirping, the wind brushing across your skin, the stars twinkling in the sky. Watch the fireflies blinking in the night and hear the frogs croaking. Feel your dog resting by your feet. Breathe deeply, take it all in, and sense this energy uniting everything around you. Feel it radiating through your body as you imagine the same life energy flowing through all of this, and through you.

Now try something else. The next time you look at other people, imagine that you share the exact same spirit with them, the only difference being your physical appearance. Imagine you are looking into a mirror and seeing a different version of yourself. When you walk past them on the street and say hello, imagine that you are greeting yourself. Or when you encounter someone disabled, imagine your shared spirit is also within them, only this time experiencing a whole different set of physical challenges. When you see a hungry child, recognize your spirit within them and that your body is starving for something to eat. Maybe even imagine yourself in the position of a powerful person helping others, or perhaps as someone greedy, exploiting others for personal gain. Think of your spirit in the form of an abused person—or even the abuser? As you do these things think of the oneness, the unity, of you connected with everyone and everything around you.

Take it even further: Look deep into nature. Envision your spirit in the form of an abandoned dog about to be euthanized, or in the bees pollinating flowers in your garden. Feel yourself in trees, in the birds, in the grass and the sun's energy casting across your skin.

I'm not just suggesting this as a theoretical idea. I'm suggesting we are not individual souls, but instead, there is only one divine spirit, or one soul. This mysterious energy that exists in us, and everything, is one spirit, the Holy Spirit of God, manifested in infinite forms, within each and every one of us, and throughout all of creation. If we viewed life this way, we would value things very differently, act with more compassion, and develop a deeper sense of empathy, respect, and appreciation for all of creation. In fact, it would change the world if we saw ourselves in everything around us. We wouldn't see anyone as better or worse than anyone else. We would honor what we consume and care for our planet.

All of a sudden, feeling this new connectedness, I'm experiencing a greater sense of love for everything than ever before. Now as I concentrate on this life energy within, feeling the spirit in me with a greater vibrancy than ever. Feeling this vibrancy radiating from me, through me, and connecting with everything around me as one infinite spiritual energy. As I stand in my backyard at night gazing at the stars I feel it radiating throughout the universe. All of a sudden I feel at one with my dog, the trees, the crickets and even the air I breathe. This connectedness gives me a new sense of responsibility to all that is around me. It's even affected my relationships and how I view and interact with others. Now, as I walk down the street and greet people, I no longer think of them as strangers. Instead I feel them as connected brothers and sisters. Even though their life experience is very different from mine, I see myself in them and in that way feel a oneness I had not known before. The more I concentrate on our connectedness, the less I'm influenced by appearances of our racial, sexual or social status differences. Even more powerful, among my

relationships with friends and family, I sense a deeper soulmate connection than ever. Looking into their eyes is like looking through windows into their soul and, recognizing we share the same divine spirit, I feel a deeper bond of love than I've ever known. I feel a new sense of love, compassion, empathy and responsibility to care for them and the world around me. It brings new meaning for me about when Jesus said, "Love your neighbor as yourself".

So, my spirit is God in me and everything around me! Totally connected like one giant network of spiritual energy flowing through me and all of existence! This connection with everything around me brings a new sense of love and appreciation for it all.

<u>Sensing love leads me to ask, "Where do these emotions come from?"</u>

Everything I've written so far has focused on the fundamental 'structures' of existence and how it operates—by observing the smallest components of matter and drawing parallels to how creation functions. I've been inspired by subatomic particles and the mysterious energy that binds atoms and molecules together, energy that, like the universe and God, is eternal. This energy fuels nature and the cosmos, as well as our feelings, awareness, consciousness, spirit, and soul. I've theorized that this energy is the one shared spirit of God manifesting in all of creation. While that's an interesting concept, something is still missing. It attempts to describe God, but it still doesn't address the essence of God.

So, I began to meditate on the question: "What IS this energy?" In doing so, I began to focus on the sensation of this energy within me and the first question that came to mind was "What does it feel like?" I know it's real and alive because I feel it in everything. I've been assuming that it might be spirit or soul, but what *is* it? Science refers to it as an electromagnetic force, but that's merely a physics description of the phenomenon. It doesn't tell me anything about the essence of it. I sense something far more mysterious and magical than that! Since everything I've sensed about this life energy spirit comes from a feeling, is the essence of it linked to 'emotions'?

Are emotions, God?

Now I'm even more curious about *love*! I'm beginning to see it in ways I never have before.

As I sit here, focusing on my dog sleeping peacefully at my feet, basking in the warmth of the love between us, I find myself filled with questions. Where does love come from? What is it, truly? I feel this emotion called 'love,' but could it also be a form of energy? Could this 'magical energy force' and our emotions actually be one and the same? What exactly *are* emotions, and where do they originate—my brain, my heart? We know they're real because we experience them, but where do these emotions come from?

I find myself thinking again about atomic energy, the mysterious force that binds particles together. Could this energy be a life force—or even a soul, or God within us? If emotions and consciousness are also inexplicable forces, could it be that this energy manifests itself as our feelings or senses? And if so, might God, whom we often think of as a deity, actually be a universal spiritual power, embodied in the form of an emotion? If that's true, then the energy within me might actually be a divine power driven by emotions, a force binding together the atoms that make up who I am.

For instance, as I mentioned earlier, there's research involving flatworms that suggests memory might be stored not just in the brain but also in the energy of their atomic structure. If that's the case, could it also be that emotions, too, are stored in this energy? And if this energy is eternal, does that mean the emotions I feel never die? If my dog and I are connected by the same spirit, does that mean the love we share is eternal, too? And in considering that, am I forgetting that we aren't two separate spirits, but rather one spirit in two different incarnations? In that light, is the love I feel for my dog actually me loving myself? Or more profoundly, is this love between us God loving God, delighting in this particular expression of creation?*

Is Love all there is?

Are emotions 'God'? Could this mysterious power that drives and binds all of Creation actually be emotions? Is this power 'God'—living in me, my dog, and everything around us? Curiously, I remember the Bible saying, "God is love. Whoever lives in love lives in God, and God in them" (John 4:8). While this passage resonates with me, I want to clarify that neither the Bible nor any other religious texts brought me to these reflections. All of these thoughts have come through meditation and prayer with my dog.

As I meditate more deeply on this concept of love, I begin to perceive it as something far more profound and powerful than I ever have before. This reflection leads me to consider other emotions—happiness, sadness, hatred, anger, greed, desire, pride. But here's where things get complicated. These emotions are real too, yet many of them are not desirable. If we equate love with God, must we also equate hate with God? That doesn't sit right with me; I cannot accept that God is hate.

And then, a stunning realization dawns on me: Love is the *only* emotion! Every other emotion is simply a reaction to love. It's all about positive and negative forces again. Think about it—happiness comes from having what you love; sadness arises from losing what you love. Hate is the opposition to love, anger comes from being denied something you love, greed and desire stem from wanting something you love, and pride emerges from basking in something you love. Every emotion ties back to love! Love, then, is the single omnipresent force behind all of Creation!

This new understanding transforms my perception of love. I used to think of it as a fleeting, pleasurable feeling. Now I see love as the most powerful force there is—an energy that shapes everything, all emotions, and all of Creation. *God is Love.*

<u>If God is Love, and Love is everything, what about evil? Does this mean God can also be evil?</u>

This leads me to a deeper, more complicated question about love. On one hand, all of creation is so magnificent and beautiful, but on the other hand, why does evil exist? If love is everything, does that mean love can be evil? And if God is love, could that mean God is also evil? Why was Jesus crucified? What about Hitler, pedophiles, and domestic abusers? Why do we, as human beings, lie, hate, cheat, and steal? If, as I've suggested, we're all expressions of the same divine spirit—that we are, in essence, God—does that mean Hitler was God? That Pilate, who murdered Jesus, was God? What about abusers, are they God? Does God commit acts of hatred, dishonesty, and violence? Why would a loving God allow such things to happen?

Some would argue that these evils are not of God, but of Satan. But I struggle with that idea too, because it suggests there's another divine power in creation. Many people believe in a cosmic battle between God and Satan—good vs. evil—and that we're all occasionally influenced by evil. But as I pray on this, I don't feel there's more than one deity at work. I still feel that this energy I've been calling God, or Love, is the one and only omnipotent power over all of creation. To suggest otherwise would be to imply that there's a part of creation beyond God's control, and that doesn't resonate with me.

So, although I don't believe in an evil deity, I'm still left wrestling with the question of duality. If there's only one God, why are there so many opposites? Time and again, the concept of positive and negative emerges. I've observed it in the charge that binds electrons to atomic nuclei. I've seen it in nature's cycles—winter to spring, night to day, death to life—and in human conditions like wealth vs. poverty, sickness vs. health, leadership vs. followership. Now, I'm seeing it in emotions: love vs. hate, happiness vs. sadness, pride vs. humility. Does this mean God embodies both good and evil, positive and negative, spiritual and material?

<u>Free will and redemption resolve the 'evil' dilemma!</u>

First, we need to define 'evil'. When we hear this word it immediately conjures up impressions of wicked, satanic beings. More correctly, evil means anything that is harmful or morally wrong.

So how does 'evil' apply to these ideas about how God uses positive / negative influences for balanced creation?

Think of *positive* as 'spiritual' energy connected with God, and *negative* as 'material' matter connected with creation. Since God requires balance, whenever one of those influences overpowers the other, the imbalance could be defined as 'evil' to the extent it has a harmful effect on balanced creation.

So, let's say 'evil' means against, or causing harm to God's vision of creation. Given that distinction, we can think of a preoccupation with material, or worldly, desires as 'evil' to the extent our 'material' desires outweigh a balanced 'spiritual' connection with God.

Bear in mind, these events are not defects in God' plan. To the contrary, this is how God works. God wants creation to evolve. This is the beauty of God's evolutionary creation. God uses evolution to correct imbalances in creation. In nature, when one species becomes overly predominant, God uses nature to correct

the imbalance. In this way, while evil is opposite of good, we can think about how God uses evil, or extremes, as a functional tool in evolutionary creation. In other words, God is never evil, or out of control. It could be said God uses this tool as a 'necessary evil' in creation.

So where does 'free will' come in?

If God is one shared spirit manifested in an infinite number of physical manifestations throughout all of creation, how can each incarnation have individual 'free will'? Think of it as a survival instinct built into everything to ensure the healthy evolution of creation. In other words, God provides 'free will' in all of material creation so it can freely evolve without God choosing every outcome.

In nature, 'free will' is the instinct that drives that seagull to take that baby turtle. Likewise, 'free will' is the instinct that drives competition for male dominance in procreation of their species. God doesn't consciously control which animals succeed and which fail. But in this way, God's vision allows nature to freely evolve in a perpetual state of creation. In the animal and plant world, 'free will' seems to be more of a balanced ecological system of taking only what's needed for survival. In this way, I believe animals maintain a natural connection with God that is quite different from that of humans. In nature, unlike in humans, I don't believe 'evil' obsessions play much of a role in nature.

Human 'free will' tends to be more complicated. We're driven by interests, talents, emotions and ambition to make choices that can be, in many ways, either good or bad for our species.

On one hand, our 'free will' produces positive outcomes for the survival of our species. Our 'free will' motivates us to pursue personal interests. We make beautiful things, provide opportunities for others to thrive, innovate solutions to problems, inspire compassion, provide education, healthcare solutions, enjoy family, celebrate events, and build communities supported by social justice systems to ensure peaceful, safe places for us to live. When we do these things with thankfulness, a generous heart, awareness for our responsibility to creation, and a desire to fulfill a role towards the prosperity of our species, our 'free will' is acting in harmony, both spiritually and materially, with God's vision of balanced creation.

On the flip side, our personal 'free will' ambitions often lead us to 'evil' behaviors driven by selfish material desires not in balance with God's vision of creation. Unlike nature, instead of eating for survival, we eat for pleasure. We build houses with every comfort and convenience but with little regard to the effect it has on the environment. We kill animals for sport and pollute the water and air we breathe. Desire for wealth and power lead us to take advantage of others. Human 'free will' often leads us to excess, deplete resources and consume more than we need. And we often know when these extremes are influencing us in the wrong, or 'evil', direction because 'we just don't feel right about it'. For example, having a daily glass of wine doesn't negatively impact other things in life. But drinking to get a buzz every night leads to it controlling you, negatively impacting relationships and responsibilities. In this sense, it becomes 'evil' because it leads to harmful or morally wrong behaviors. In most cases, God speaks to our spiritual side, calling us to bring these 'evil' tendencies back into balance through either personal decisions or societal laws to correct the behaviors.

On a more egregious scale, human 'free will' also leads to extreme 'evil' behaviors. Lust for power leads to war and genocide where millions of innocent people are displaced, wounded and killed. Terror organizations, often driven by religious ideologies, inflict fear, death and destruction to justify their beliefs on others. Sexual predators, consumed by sick mental perversions, prey on women and children. Greed leads to crime, fraud, drug addiction, violence and even slavery. At this level, 'evil' is so extreme and pervasive it infects society as a whole. Here's where it feels like an evil deity is at work in the world. If I don't believe in an evil deity, for what purpose does God allow things to get this far out of control? Again, the answer goes back to, it's how God works. It's the balance of negative and positive influences to allow evolutionary creation. Here is how 'communities' play a role.

God is not 'evil' because God is not consciously creating these situations. God's vision for creation is to allow 'free will' so that creation can evolve naturally on its own. Sometimes one species tries to overcome another. Every species has built in mechanisms for correcting destructive excesses. Think of these as community defense mechanisms. For example: Polio is a highly infectious virus leading to paralysis and death that was a serious global health threat until we developed a vaccine to bring it under control. In the case of 'evil' human behaviors, we have societal justice systems that give us the tools to respond, mitigate and defeat these threats. These egregious 'evil' behaviors present themselves to inspire human society to develop methods to protect humanity. As a society, it is our moral obligation to hold those guilty who commit these crimes against humanity. In this way, we are God's tools for preserving the balance of spiritual / material influences that support the healthy evolution of our species.

I'm having lots of thoughts regarding how we resolve these choices. For now, I'll just say God provides 'free will' as a survival instinct built into all of material creation so it can freely evolve without God choosing every outcome. This leads to potential excesses that overcome our spiritual connection to God. When this happens these behaviors can be considered morally harmful, or 'evil', to the extent it is our moral responsibility to correct them. This leads to a more nuanced discussion about redemption or salvation which can be explored later. But for now, I'm focusing only on the question of resolving 'evil' as it relates to God and human 'free will'.

<u>Does God have a plan, or conscious intent?</u>

This discussion about 'free will' leads me to think more deeply about, to what extent does God consciously influence outcomes? Is it random? Like put things in place and let chips fall where they may? Is it controlled chaos?

While at first these questions feel unsettling, the more I meditate on the idea that God uses creative evolution to manifest existence, the more comfortable I am with it. Although God may not have a predetermined plan, there is conscious intent at work—an intention to use balance in creation. God isn't a deity that plans and directs the outcome of everything. I'm reminded, the very definition of creation, in a divine sense, is the act of bringing the universe or life into being as a manifestation of divine will. It is a process of producing something new, such as a work of art, a piece of writing, or an invention. Creation is an evolution of a vision, not a predetermined result. God isn't something separate from creation, *God is Creation!*

In my heart, how do I know this to be true? The answer is so obvious it's living right inside of me! I have conscious awareness and visions for things I want to create. I know that to be real! And it seems to me there can be no other explanation for where that comes from other than, it must be the power of God in me! So, as I reflect on this, I believe that makes me living proof for how God works, because when I create something, that's how I work!

When I begin a creative project, I start with a conscious vision of the desired outcome. I use tools that I believe will help me reach that result, and I guide the process—but I don't control it completely. As I create a piece of artwork it evolves organically through the interaction of the materials I use. If I try to force it too much, I end up fighting the process, and the artwork can become overworked. My best results come when I align with my vision and allow the natural flow of the materials to influence the outcome. By the end, I might be pleased with what I've created, and I will also have learned new techniques to use in the future. Since I create with conscious intent, and I believe that the spirit within me is actually God working through me, then I understand that God also creates with conscious intent. God uses me as a vessel to manifest a vision, just as God does in all of creation. God is the artist, experimenting with universal elements to achieve evolutionary creation.

In other words, what might look like chaos is really the evolutionary process of creation. Consider this: if you plant two seeds, one in rich soil and the other in poor soil, both will take root. But neither seed knows what it will become. One will grow deep roots and produce many flowers, while the other will struggle to survive. Both seeds are the same, but the conditions they were planted in shaped their outcomes.

God freely allowing creation to manifest into a harmonious existence is the awesome beauty of it all!

<u>We need inspiration to grow!</u>

Viewing the world in this way, it becomes easier to see how everything evolves in response to the environment it's in. You're more likely to be wealthy if you grow up in a wealthy family. You're more likely to be successful if you surround yourself with successful people. If you have a strong education, you're more likely to have a thriving career. If you grow up in poverty, you're more likely to remain poor. If you live in unhealthy conditions, you're more prone to illness.

Taking it a step further, if it's true that God is the one living spirit within all of us, why don't we all share the exact same intelligence, insights or talents! If the same spirit of God is in all of us, why are some people prodigies like Einstein or Mozart, while others struggle with basic skills? Why are some born leaders while others are naturally followers? If the same spirit of God is also within my dog, why doesn't my dog think exactly as I do?

Once again, the concept of creative growth through balanced evolution becomes evident. We need inspiration to inspire and motivate us to achieve new achievements. Both leaders and followers are necessary

for the stability of society. Mozart's music elevates our spirits, inspiring creativity, while Einstein challenges us to push the boundaries of knowledge and understanding. Although some may achieve greatness, despite our circumstances, we all have unique abilities. It's up to each of us to find them, and put them to work in our lives. For example, even my dog has her own unique perspective, she plays a role essential to our relationship and her own species, and contributes in ways that may not align with human thought but are vital nonetheless.

God isn't replicated in us. We are each unique
expressions of God!

God transcends all creation in ways we cannot fully
comprehend. Rather than seeing the same spirit of God
replicated in each of us, it's more expansive to view God
as an omnipresence permeating all of existence,
expressing itself through us. Imagine God's presence as
rays of sunlight shining through different windows in a
house. The universe is the house, we are the windows,
and each beam of light represents a unique
manifestation of God.

God doesn't merely replicate in each of us but instead
expresses different aspects of the divine to serve
creation's greater evolution. Each of us—whether
human, animal, or plant—plays a unique role. My dog
doesn't know what I know because she doesn't need to.
She knows what she needs to fulfill her role as a dog.
Likewise, I don't need to know what she knows or what
my best friend knows to fulfill my part in creation. Bees
know what they need to make honey and keep their
species going, just as every
other creature knows what is
necessary for their part in the
cosmic design. Collectively, we
are all unique expressions of
God, contributing to the
creative evolution of the
universe!

IV. LOVE IS GOD

So far, this meditation, or prayer, has been a journey to find God. It started with a curiosity about my dog's relationship to God which transcended to all of creation. It led me to concentrate on the emotional energies flowing between us and made me question the nature of that energy. This made me think of how all of existence, including me and my dog, is made up of atoms surrounded by positive / negative energy forces that can never be destroyed. Fascinated by this magical, mysterious infinite energy I began to sense it might be, not only our spirits, but the one living spirit of God manifested in an infinite number of ways throughout creation. Imagining this could be God, it led me to questions about free-will, self-awareness, consciousness, good vs. evil, divine justice and emotions. I needed to imagine how all of existence could be one Spirit, or God, with a conscious vision for creation, while still allowing everything to freely evolve. Understanding how positive / negative, or Spiritual / Material forces work towards balanced evolution helps me contemplate how God works in all of this. But one final question keeps nagging at me.

I'm still curious about the 'essence' of this mysterious infinite energy that permeates everything. Where does it come from? It feels as though these intangible energies like self-awareness, consciousness, free-will, memories and emotions are a living force within us. But what is it? A feeling? A thought? An energy? A Spirit?

Meditating deeply on this, I look again at my dog sleeping at my feet. I can feel the sensation of love flowing between us. And it occurs to me the actual nature of this mystical, 'magical energy' I've been talking about throughout this chapter is actually 'LOVE'! And if this eternal living spirit in everything is God, then God is Love! My first thought after thinking this is, 'Really? After all this, I'm just concluding what every preacher always says, "God is Love!"! But no, this is different. Like some sort of epiphany, it feels like I'm awakening to a new revelation of Love! It's like I'm seeing Love for the first time in my life in a way that I never dreamed existed!

This is something so powerful, I can't say it in words. You have to feel it!

Try it yourself! You can't think about this. You have to pray, or meditate on it. Maybe sit with your dog, focus on that energy of love flowing between you. Concentrate on that feeling of love as a mysterious energy force flowing through both your body and that of your dog. It's not just a feeling. It's alive! A real living power coming from somewhere. Not your heart, or your brain... it's Love, living in your Soul!

Love is the essence of God living in you and everything around you!

And here's why I believe this! Reflecting on my earlier discussion, *'Is Love all there is?'*... a stunning realization dawns on me: Love is the *only* emotion!" Every other emotion is simply a reaction to love. It's all about positive and negative forces again. Think about it— happiness comes from having what you love; sadness arises from losing what you love. Hate is the opposition to love, anger comes from being denied something you love, greed and desire stem from wanting something you love, and pride emerges from basking in something you love. Every emotion ties back to love! Love, then, is the single omnipresent force behind all of Creation! This new understanding transforms my perception of love. I used to think of it as a fleeting, pleasurable feeling. Now I see love as the most powerful force there is—an energy that shapes everything, all emotions, and all of Creation. *It's not just God is Love. It's better to say, Love is God!*

For the first time in life, I can say I truly believe in God! I feel God everywhere! As I look around me, think about my dog, the plants, the trees, my family, friends, interests and basically everything in my life I become aware the core feeling or drive related to all of it, in an infinite number of ways, is Love! I feel connected to everything like never before! I feel at one with my dog, all of nature, the stars, the universe all buzzing with a living spiritual energy, alive with love and striving to live and evolve. Like one surging river of Love surging through everything! This is God!

The implications of this are profound! If we truly are the same spirit manifesting through different forms, we would recognize ourselves in others! Like dressing up in two costumes—despite the external differences, we would still recognize ourselves in both. Imagine the transformation if we could see ourselves as the same spirit living through countless incarnations. Recognizing ourselves in others would erase racism and sexism. Seeing ourselves in animals would end cruelty towards them. Acknowledging ourselves in nature would drive us to treat the earth with care. Seeing ourselves in the poor or disabled would grow our compassion, and recognizing our shared spirit in those overwhelmed by sorrow would deepen our empathy and desire to bring them happiness. It's like the saying, "put yourself in their shoes." If we could truly see ourselves in everything, the world would be reshaped by love, compassion, and understanding. If we feel God inside us, feel God in everything around us, we will see ourselves in everything. We'd be more grateful for the blessings of life and inspired for our place in it all!

Maybe this is what is meant when the Bible says, *'God is love. Whoever lives in love lives in God, and God in them' (John 4:16).* God is this eternal, ever-expanding mass of energy, a universal power driven by infinite love. Just as there is no beginning and no end, there is no birth and no death. Everything has always been and always will be. All manifestations of God are in a forever state of growing and evolving as one omnipresent manifestation of God. We, and everything, are God!

God is not some deity we might meet some day if we're good! God is right in front of us, inside of us, and on divine display in the universe all around us! God isn't just with us! God is in us! We are God, manifesting God's dream of creation!

As I said in the first paragraph... "I'm pretty certain my dog never contemplates God. Watching her lie peacefully in the grass, I ponder what goes on in her mind. .... The concepts of God, spirit, life's purpose, or eternity never cross her mind. None of that matters to her. There's no need for such questions to even arise, which only deepens my curiosity about her experience."

In conclusion, maybe the most important thing I've learned from this journey is you don't have to know or believe anything about any of this to find God! Finding God is a personal experience that we each discover in our own way. So, if you also find yourself on a similar journey and looking for ways to connect with God, the thing I found that worked the best for me was to... ***"Pray with your dog!"***

CHAPTER
FOUR

Prayer

CONNECTING
WITH GOD!

4 | PRAYER
"Connecting With God!"

U p until now, I can't honestly say I ever truly believed in prayer. While I've said many prayers throughout my life, they often felt like a ritualistic obligation, rather than something I genuinely believed would connect me with God.

That began to change in this experience with my dog!

I know many people pray with sincere, good intentions in their heart. But, I can't help but feel, when it comes to prayer, we've either lost our way or, as in my case, never really understood it in the first place. Personally, the way we are taught about it, and the way we do it, never really connected with me. It's left me with a lot of questions about prayer!

To me, human prayers always seem to be primarily motivated by selfish desires. Praying for God to give me more, solve my problems, and ask for unrepentant forgiveness. We pray for more money, a new car, and a new house. We want a better job, and to win football games. These are material human desires that don't belong in prayers to God. Like it says in the Bible, James 4:3, *"When you ask, you do not receive, because you ask with wrong motives, that you may spend what you get on your pleasures."*

People do pray for more charitable things like world peace, eliminating hunger, poverty and so on. And it's good they acknowledge and recognize these things. But too often these words are offered gratuitously. If we're going to pray for something shouldn't it be coming from deep in our hearts with a commitment to help? How often do we use prayer to feel good about doing something, while expecting God to fix the problem so we don't have to take action ourselves?

And why doesn't God answer our prayers to heal the sick and disabled? I've known very devout Christians who, along with their church, have prayed for healing. Yet I've never known any of them to get healed. Didn't Jesus say, *"if you have faith like a grain of mustard seed, you will say to this mountain, 'Move from here to there,' and it will move, and nothing will be impossible for you"*. So if that's true, did the entire devout congregation who prayed for these healings not have enough faith? What happened to God's promise?

Normally the answer I get to that question is, "when we don't get what we pray for, it's because it must not be in

God's plan". So my next question is, 'if God has a grand plan for everything, and God is going to do what God wants to do anyway, why bother with prayer?'

And what bothers me even more is repetitious prayer! "God is great, God is good...", and "Lord have mercy...", and "Bless me oh Lord..." and so on, and so on. Jesus taught against praying in vain repetitions when he said in Matthew 6:7, *"when ye pray, use not vain repetitions, as the heathens do"*. And then He gave the Lord's Prayer as a 'template' for 'how', not 'what', we should pray. Jesus said, *"This then is 'how' you should pray... Our Father who art in heaven..."*. Jesus was using it as a 'framework' for prayer. But what do we do? Even every church has us doing exactly what Jesus told us not to do! Reciting the <u>Lord's Prayer</u>, in vain repetitions as the heathens do!!!!

And then Jesus said, *"when you pray, go into your room, close the door and pray to your Father"*. In other words, prayer is something between you and God, not something that should be recited in public.

So I'm bothered by empty promises and public displays of prayer like, "I have you in my thoughts & prayers", or "let us join together in prayer", or "people waving their arms around" and social media posts with praying hands that say "Praying". I wish we wouldn't do these things in the name of prayer! It reminds of when Jesus went on to say, *"And when you pray, do not be like the hypocrites, for they love to pray standing in the synagogues and on the street corners to be seen by others"*.

Don't get me wrong, I know people are expressing true heartfelt sentiments when they do these things. But I'm trying to make a distinction between expressing sentiments and calling it prayer because I think it demonstrates how much we trivialize prayer. If it's not about sincere, reverent prayer to God, I don't think we should be calling it prayer! So for all those reasons, I choose not to recite the Lord's Prayer, or join in with any group or public prayers.

All of this makes me think about how weary God must become of humans constantly pleading for more! Imagine getting flooded with billions of prayer requests like this every minute of every day! All contradicting each other because one person's wishes would be in conflict with others. All of this focus on material requests and public displays feels empty, superficial, disingenuous and irreverent. It leaves me feeling most people, including most clergy, don't know the first thing about prayer! Prayer should be a much more introspective, personal experience than all of that.

As I consider these questions about prayer, I'm reminded of Jesus in the Garden of Gethsemane. His prayer was the opposite of shallow or materialistic—he was in such earnest connection with God that he began to sweat blood. This extreme example makes me question: what is true prayer supposed to be?

Prayer is a process of aligning our hearts and minds with God's will. In prayer, we are not simply presenting a wish list; we are engaging in a dialogue with the divine, seeking intimacy with God. It's about being in God's presence, experiencing His love and guidance, and growing spiritually. The more I meditate on this, the more I find myself experiencing a much deeper reflection on prayer.

So, 'what is prayer?'

While pondering this question, I look at my dog again. I'm noticing her state of peace seems so different than all the thoughts circling around in my brain. She's probably not thinking about anything. Just noticing all the sounds I'm not even aware of. Recognizing the unique scents of dozens of different smells I can't smell. She seems happy, peaceful, relaxed, and content. No cares. Not wondering about what's next. Just taking it all in. Hearing, feeling nature. Not praying. Knowing she's part of it all.

Animals don't pray for food or shelter. Plants don't pray for water. With the exception of humans, the rest of the natural world seemingly just goes about life accepting what's given and experiencing their place in it all.

Does the rest of nature feel God simply as a sensation, or stream of consciousness, or life energy of which they are a part? Maybe they don't need to consciously bring their minds, or energies, into a state of prayer. Maybe consciousness isn't even the right word because I doubt if plants share conscious awareness in the same way we think of it. That said, there must be something to their awareness because we do know they possess energy responses to stimuli. I believe nature is connected to God on a level I'm not plugged into. They don't even think about God. They have no need to pray because they seem naturally connected to everything. They are not separate from it, they are it. And they don't think about God, because God is just part of their being.

So, maybe nature doesn't pray to God, or think about God, because there is no need to. They seem so much more naturally connected to the eternal stream of life than I am. I know they have awareness of nature, and instincts that drive how they fit into everything. But I don't think they need to dwell on the existence of God because they are naturally connected to God's conscious intent for them. So, in a sense, I believe nature does experience a state of prayer, or communication with God, because God is just in them. As if God is just there whispering to them as they take in creation while feeling their part in it all.

So I have to ask myself why are humans the only creatures who feel the need to consciously pray to God? Could it be that our minds are so busy with the material aspects of life that we are more disconnected than nature, so we need prayer to reconnect?

As I dwell on these thoughts I'm feeling more curious about entering a state of meditative prayer. I know I need to let go of the busyness in my brain and let my mind drift. To help me do that I divert my attention to the trees all around me reaching to a sunlit sky. I think about them standing there quietly in one place for decades. I think about the life energy flowing through them and wonder about what kind of awareness or consciousness they must possess that allows them to stand in one place, year after year. There must be a sense of wisdom and peace that comes with that.

The more I concentrate on this I notice all the material matters in my mind falling away. I'm now sensing that flow of living energy within me more strongly than before. I'm feeling more connected to everything. Me, the trees, my dog, everything is part of it all like one giant energy force permeating everything.

I'm becoming more aware of an elevated state of spiritual communication. It feels sort of like a spiritual energy flowing through me like a river and everything around me. Or, a heightened awareness of my connection to all of creation. Like finding a new channel or wavelength where we are all one shared spirit. The one shared spirit of God manifested through us in infinite ways.

I'm trying to describe an experience that makes me feel a sense of prayer more strongly than ever before. It's as if I've connected with my true eternal self with no dependency on the physical me. Which is leading me to feel a real connection with God. As if God is speaking to me silently in a stream of consciousness within my soul. It's a warm, safe, comfortable sense of being. It makes me want to stay here. But I know there is more to my purpose than to just live in a state of meditation.

I become more aware of the differences between my material interests and my spiritual interests. I better understand how my material needs draw my attention from my spiritual state of consciousness.

And the more I think about this 'material' vs. 'spiritual' dynamic, it occurs to me how it also translates to the idea of 'sin' vs. 'salvation'! This elevated state of connection to the spiritual, is making me more aware of how my material desires interfere with my ability to connect at this level. It occurs to me, in this context, we could think of the material as 'sin' to the extent it is creating an imbalance from the spiritual, or God.

I remember a preacher once saying that 'sin' meant separation from God. That comes to mind as this prayer, or meditation, experience I'm having is deepening my interest in the dynamic between spiritual and material forces. It leads me to reflect on how material and spiritual forces might relate to the concepts of sin and salvation. For example, if sin means separation from God, then I can relate sin to the material. When we focus too much on material things, we are pulled away from a deeper spiritual connection to God. So, in this sense, sin isn't just about evil as we often think of it. Instead, sin, like material desires, is about separation from God. It's not that material things are inherently bad, but they become "sinful" to the extent that they disconnect us from our spiritual awareness.

So, in this way, sin isn't some grand cosmic evil but rather the imbalance that occurs when our material desires outweigh our connection to God. In other words, material desires can equal sin to the degree at which they interfere with our spiritual consciousness.

Salvation, then, becomes the process of restoring that balance—aligning our material desires with our spiritual awareness so we can live in harmony with God's purpose for us. So, rather than viewing sin simply as 'evil,' we can see it as the extent to which material concerns overpower our spiritual connection. It's about balancing both forces to live out God's vision for our lives.

How we navigate that balance would be a deeper meditation about Salvation. But for now, since I'm focusing on prayer, it's important to remember the essential role prayer can play in salvation is about how it brings us back to that spiritual connection in our daily lives. So all of this underscores the importance of meditative prayer in our lives!

I don't believe we need to be praying every waking moment but we should be mindful of keeping a 'prayerful' state. It makes me think of other eastern and native American theological traditions. While they all have different practices, they similarly relate to the importance of prayer as a way to connect with a higher power, nature, or the divine energy that flows through all life. They all share a focus on balance, meditation, and the integration of prayer into daily life. Prayer is not just about asking for things, but about aligning oneself with a greater spiritual force, whether that's God, the Tao, or the Great Spirit.

I've found I can keep this state of mind even while doing simple things like walking my dog. Taking advantage of private moments like this gives me a chance to spiritually reflect on how best to deal with the material issues I need to face today. How I should treat people I need to deal with. How love and respect needs to overpower my need to 'win' the day. I try to recognize my impulsive behaviors so I can open myself to listening to others with an open heart. I think about issues facing others and reflect on how to be helpful without being manipulative. I remind myself it's better to be humble and loving without being judgmental. I try to let go of wanting to take charge of deciding what's best for everyone. I try to focus on putting myself in another's shoes, to listen and learn about where they are coming from. To really understand their needs, concerns and interests and then ask myself how I can contribute in that way.

This is an example of keeping spiritually mindful of all these things as I go about daily life. In doing so, my prejudices and personal desires dissipate, helping me to keep my daily agendas spiritually guided to harmonize with the natural world and maintain a balance between the material and spiritual realms.

On reflection, in the beginning of this chapter I may have been too critical of prayer. Although I believe my critique on praying for material things is relevant, it's not for me, or anyone else to judge what prayer should or shouldn't be. That is between each individual and their personal relationship to God. The important thing is that we pray with our hearts. Prayer is not us talking to God, it is connecting to the spirit of God living within us! Put another way, it's like us talking to us, our inner spiritual selves, because our inner spirits are actually the spirit of God living within us.

My motivation for writing this chapter was to share revelations that have restored my faith and understanding about the value of prayer. As I prayed, or meditated, on these things I can honestly say I feel as though, for the first time in my life, I actually felt the experience of communicating with God. I feel blessed to be able to say, I now know what it feels like to speak with God. Not in a voice but with something inside me that felt like I was hearing it. It's amazing to me that a simple thing like sitting and meditating with

your dog can lead someone to so many profound enlightenments about God's creation. Up until now, my relationship with God had more to do with things I was taught as opposed to something I felt. But now, for the first time in my life, I can say I truly believe in God. This experience has changed my understanding as to how prayer keeps me connected with the living spirit of God within me.

Now recognizing that the living spirit within us is actually God, whenever I want to see God, all I need to do is look into the eyes of my dog. I tell her to sit and look into my eyes. Looking up at me with her beautiful deep brown eyes, like looking through windows to her soul, I see her living spirit staring back at me. I feel the spirit of God in her and recognize it as the same spirit of God living in me. It leaves me feeling grateful, loving, and blessed knowing her, and me, and everything around us are connected, each of us, as our own unique manifestation of God's dream of creation!

So whenever you want to feel connected with the Spirit of God, I suggest trying what always works for me!

"Pray with your dog!"

CHAPTER
FIVE

Salvation

LIVING
MY BEST LIFE!

5 | SALVATION

"A New Way to Think About 'Sin' and 'Salvation'!"

My journey to find God began with moments sitting beside my dog, where I felt a powerful, loving energy flowing between us. Feeling this emotion as a real, living energy we both shared led me to wonder about its origin. Where was this coming from? Through prayer and meditation, I began to sense that this feeling of 'love' was more than just an emotion—it felt like a divine spiritual energy. The more I reflected, the more I realized that this energy was not just present between me and my dog, but woven into all of existence. I sensed it was present in everything around us! The squirrels, the bees, the grass, the trees! It dawned on me: this feeling of love is actually God, living in everything like an infinite, unifying force that permeates all creation. Suddenly, I found myself believing that 'Love' is the foundational divine energy of creation itself. That 'Love' is the spiritual energy of God present in everything!

In this newfound awareness, I began to see all of existence as divided into two realms: the spiritual, as the eternal energy of God that exists in everything, and the material world, which is God manifesting evolutionary creation in an infinite variety of forms. I started to realize we aren't merely connected to God; everything is God, each of us playing out unique roles in this grand creation. This means God is everything—both spiritual and material.

Yet, as I reflected more on the complexities of living my material life, I realized how the demands of my physical needs pull me away from spiritual awareness. How the desires of material existence, by their nature, overshadow my connection to the spirit within me. But I didn't see this as wrong because living in the physical world, by design, requires us to focus on providing for our material needs. God created things this way! By design, God's divine plan requires free evolution of creation in order for it to thrive.

This new sense of the divine led me to start thinking about how this all might relate to other theological concepts I grew up with, like 'evil,' 'sin,' 'redemption,' and 'salvation.' How do my new ideas of God as an omnipresent loving energy that permeates everything fit within this picture? It led me to start thinking of these things very differently. Instead of thinking of actions as 'evil,' I began considering the essence of so-called 'sin' as meaning a spiritual separation from God—not through moral failing but through distraction by our physical needs.

So If 'Sin' Isn't 'Evil,' Why Do We Need Salvation?

Since I believe there is only one all-powerful God, it follows that Satan doesn't exist. Likewise, neither would 'evil' or 'sin'—at least not as I've traditionally understood those things. Yet wrongdoing and moral failings do exist. So rather than think of these as 'evil' acts, I began to think of them as 'sinful' only in the sense that they represent material desires overcoming the spiritual. In this way, 'sin' takes on a new meaning: it is not so much evil wrongdoing but rather separation from spiritual enlightenment. So, the idea of Salvation is not so much about seeking God's forgiveness. Rather, Salvation becomes the act of reconciling the imbalance of pursuing material desires over spiritual connectedness.

But Why Would God Create a System That Allows Material Needs to Interfere With Spiritual Connections?

On the contrary, the exact opposite is true! Actually, it's this dynamic of how God allows material existence to freely evolve that is so amazingly perfect! To us, when things seemingly go wrong, we often view them as failures. But if we step back and view them differently, more in context with how evolutionary creation works, we might then see them from a new perspective. We begin to understand that everything happens with purpose. Even amongst all this seemingly chaotic activity, everything always operates within orderly rules of evolutionary transitions. Every action has a reaction.

There's life, death, and rebirth. Infinite processes that evolve, grow, and change, manifesting in countless relationships.

For example, in an age of constant connectivity, we can become preoccupied with our phones, social media, or endless entertainment. These distractions often pull us away from being present with our loved ones or even ourselves. The balance comes in recognizing the difference between when technology serves us versus when it enslaves us. This extreme makes us mindful of the negative impact distractions have on our relationships. Salvation occurs when we consciously adjust these habits in order to foster stronger personal connections.

This amazing interplay between chaos and order reflects how divine creation unfolds. Even when we perceive failure, everything freely adapts in perfect harmony to fulfill God's infinite dream of eternal creation.

Living in Balance Is the Key to Salvation!

So, in this framework, from a personal perspective, I find myself redefining 'sin' not as wrongdoing but as material desires that draw me away from my spiritual self. In other words, to the degree my temporary bodily needs dominate my eternal spiritual consciousness, it causes separation from awareness of my divine purpose—or separation from God. When I prioritize material success at the expense of relationships or inner peace, I drift away from the divine connection in my soul that helps me live my best self.

At the same time, prioritizing my physical needs is absolutely right because they are necessary for my survival and growth in this existence. So, attending to them is not wrong. God wants us to attend to these needs, but these desires must be kept in balance with our spiritual purpose.

Living my best life means harmonizing these forces, allowing material pursuits to support rather than dominate my spiritual path. By always taking time to pray or meditate on my choices, I serve both my physical existence and the divine spirit within me. In doing so, I can contribute more meaningfully to God's creation by fulfilling my unique role in this infinite, evolving universe.

So although I recognize the relevance of a need for 'Salvation,' I don't think of it in terms of a path to heaven. I believe it's more like a state of grace we strive for each and every day. 'Salvation' is achieved every time I successfully reconcile the imbalance between my material desires and my spiritual conscience. In this way, Salvation means keeping me connected to, or in balance with, my divine purpose so I am able to live my best life.

Consider the person consumed by work—driven by ambition or the desire for material success, yet finding themselves estranged from family. In their pursuit of wealth, they may be unaware of the spiritual cost—the connection and love sacrificed in the process. Finding salvation here isn't about abandoning work but restoring balance, ensuring that their material goals are informed by spiritual priorities like love, presence, and nurturing relationships.

This new understanding of Salvation invites me to reflect on the many ways it applies to specific experiences in my everyday life. But because these ideas are so different from teachings I grew up with, I feel a need to honestly confront how they may, or may not, relate to, or conflict with, the teachings of my youth.

Christian literalism created obstacles for me!

Although Christianity is my background, I never believed its teachings were any more divinely inspired than those of other religions. Many other theological traditions, including some progressive Christian interpretations, more closely align with my new revelations about 'sin' and 'salvation.' Like all religions, I see Christian teachings as divinely inspired philosophical and theological writings—but I don't believe in their literal interpretations. While I respect their inherent messages, these teachings created obstacles that actually prevented me from connecting with God. Yet, because I do believe there is divine

inspiration in those stories, I'm curious about how they might resonate with my new relationship with God.

The Challenge of 'Evil' and 'Sin'

First, I never believed in Satan or an evil deity. I've always believed in one all-powerful, omnipresent deity. However, this belief presented a dilemma because, clearly, so-called 'evil' exists. How could there be evil in a world created by an all-loving God?

I couldn't ignore the concept of 'sin' as separation from God through 'evil' acts, but I struggled to understand its origin. If there is only one God, how could evil coexist with divine perfection? These questions haunted me and left me searching for a deeper understanding of what 'evil' truly is.

The Story of Original Sin

I never believed creation happened in seven days. I was taught that Adam and Eve committed original sin when they disobeyed God and ate from the Tree of Knowledge. This act supposedly separated them from God, and their sin was passed down to all humankind. We are, according to this teaching, born guilty of this 'original sin' and must seek forgiveness and salvation to reunite with God.

Metaphorically, I understand the idea that human desires separate us from God. But why would God give us free will and then expect us not to seek knowledge? Why place the Tree of Knowledge in the garden at all?

I've never believed God feels the need to test us with temptation. If God allows temptation, does that mean God also allows evil? That idea conflicts with the concept of a perfect creation.

While I sensed a valuable 'reconciliation' message in this story, its literal interpretation didn't resonate with my personal experience. To me, the story of the fall of humankind became meaningful only when viewed as a metaphor for the inevitable struggle between spiritual and material existence.

The Idea of Salvation

Even more troubling was the notion that salvation required the cruel blood sacrifice of Jesus as payment for humanity's sins. According to fundamental Christianity, we must pray for forgiveness, accept Jesus as our Lord and Savior, and be rewarded with eternal life. Otherwise, we face eternal damnation.

What kind of all-loving God would devise such a plan? Why would a benevolent Creator require suffering and sacrifice to redeem humanity? This interpretation seemed twisted and inconsistent with the God of love I believed in. Worse still, it suggested that our relationship with God should be based on fear rather than love.

Shouldn't I want to follow Jesus' teachings because they represent the right way to live, not because of the promise of heaven or fear of hell? These questions deepened my disconnect from fundamental Christianity, even as I continued to search for meaning within its teachings.

Seeking Broader Perspectives

To be fair, there is no absolute right or wrong way to think about God. None of us possess ultimate truth or knowledge about the divine. Literal Christian teachings may be as valid for others as my interpretations are for me. What matters is seeking God in our hearts and embracing the personal relationship that emerges.

I've also come to appreciate the progressive Christian view that these stories function as metaphors rather than historical accounts. They offer insights into free will and the tension between spiritual and material existence. This perspective aligns more closely with my own evolving understanding of God, sin, and salvation.

Other Influences on My Spiritual Journey

While Christianity shaped much of my early understanding, my journey to find God has spanned decades and drawn inspiration from many traditions, teachings, and experiences. Here are some that profoundly influenced my spiritual awakening:

- *Tarot Cards:* The Major Arcana captivated me with vivid depictions of the human journey toward spiritual awakening. Each card mirrored steps we take to connect with life's mysteries and move closer to God.

- *Hinduism, Buddhism, and Kabbalah:* Though I never studied these traditions in depth, their teachings on balancing material and spiritual existence resonated deeply with me. They reinforced the idea that material desires often obscure spiritual truths.

- *Carlos Castaneda:* His writings introduced me to alternate dimensions of spiritual awareness, inspiring me to explore truths beyond the tangible world.

- *The Prophet by Kahlil Gibran:* The chapter "On Love," which profoundly shaped my understanding of divine love as a connection to all creation.

- *Jonathan Livingston Seagull by Richard Bach:* This story of a seagull breaking free from worldly constraints inspired me to seek the freedom and beauty of spiritual connection.

- *The Celestine Prophecy by James Redfield:* Its focus on the spiritual and material interplay encouraged me to recognize the divine design in all things.

- *Hawaiian Ho'oponopono:* Its emphasis on resolving conflicts and repairing connections resonated with my view of salvation as reconnecting with God and healing separations caused by material desires.

- *Mutant Message Down Under by Marlo Morgan:* This transformative journey with an Aboriginal tribe taught me the importance of interconnectedness and the rejection of materialism.

Each of these influences enriched my journey. Unlike fundamental Christianity, none of them claimed to be the sole path to God. This openness encouraged me to explore spiritual truths from many perspectives.

Back to Jesus, Beyond Literalism

Christian exclusivity created barriers for me. The idea that salvation is achievable only through accepting Jesus as Lord and Savior felt unnecessarily divisive. If so many traditions agree on the principles of moral responsibility, human choice, and spiritual enlightenment, why should Christianity claim exclusivity?

This led me to question the literal story of Jesus. While I respect Christianity's profound impact, its portrayal of Jesus as a sacrificial lamb doesn't resonate with me. Instead, I view Jesus' life as a metaphor for reconciling the material and the spiritual.

When Jesus said, *"I am the way, the truth, and the life,"* I interpret it as an invitation to follow his example of living harmoniously with both the divine and the human. His words, *"The kingdom of God is within you,"* remind me that we all carry the divine within us.

Even the crucifixion and resurrection hold symbolic meaning. To me, the crucifixion represents humanity's tendency to reject spiritual truths in favor of material concerns. The resurrection symbolizes the eternal nature of love and spirit, transcending the limits of physical existence. The ascension becomes the ultimate triumph of divine energy over worldly distractions.

For me, Jesus is a profound teacher and the son of God in the sense that God lives within us all. His teachings exemplify how to live a spiritually connected life in a material world. I don't need to believe every literal detail of his story to honor his message.

Now, I'm ready to move on!

To this point in this discussion I've talked about many influences that shaped my religious experiences. Beginning with fundamental Christian teaching of my youth, the obstacles it created for me to overcome, and then on to other exposures that expanded my journey into more esoteric teachings. Now I come to the point where, after all these years, I feel I've finally found a true relationship with God.

Which brings me back to my dog!

As discussed earlier, as well as, in my chapter about 'God,' these new revelations of the divine began through my relationship with my dog. Sensing the magical energy of love flowing between us, and deeply praying on its source, I experienced a spiritual connection that led me to a profound new understanding of the nature of God.

That understanding is; that 'mysterious energy' contained in everything, that binds all atomic particles of the entire universe together, is actually a divine spirit of love which is in—you, me, my dog, all of existence—we're all part of one divine manifestation of creation, connected by the singular spiritual energy of God. We are all God! We, and all of existence, are one spirit of God, constantly evolving through an infinite number of physical incarnations. We are all one in God, forever transforming, living, dying, and regenerating in an eternal evolutionary process.

So obviously, the natural extension of my spiritual journey would be incomplete without exploring deeper philosophical and theological questions about how the roles of 'sin' and 'salvation' relate, not only to humans, but to nature and _all_ of creation.

First, why do we attribute sin only to humans?

Humans are more inclined towards extreme sin because our behavior is influenced by emotions and desires that lead to overindulgence. And that sin among animals, plants and the rest of creation are more inclined towards balance because most operate within ecological limits, consuming only what they need to survive, reproduce, and thrive. So we could say the 'degree' of sin (material indulgence) is measured by how much a species takes to physically exist.

So, how does Balance, Sin, and Salvation fit in nature?

Balance (with God) - For the most part, the natural world operates in balance with creation, or God, in that it takes only what it needs to survive and doesn't require conscious efforts to connect spiritual awareness. Predators hunt only what they can eat, and plants use sunlight and nutrients in proportion to their growth requirements. Spiritually, nature exists in a constant state of connectedness with the natural world.

Sin (separation) - In nature, the idea of sin (or separation from spirit, or God) is not as extreme as it is for humans. Material consumption in nature is normally constrained to survival needs. Excess sometimes occurs when predator populations grow unchecked or invasive species are introduced, they may deplete prey or plant resources, leading to ecological imbalance. Yet, even these excesses are often naturally balanced because they can stimulate responses promoting ecological growth.

Salvation (reconciliation) - So, nature naturally reconciles imbalances by responding with built-in checks and balances (e.g., predator-prey cycles, resource competition) that prevent long-term overexploitation. Even though nature may not have conscious intent, it restores balance through natural evolutionary processes.

So, in nature, the idea of Salvation, or maintaining balance, happens by this natural cycle of resolving temporary material excess with instinctual spiritual purpose. Which naturally results in harmonious fulfillment of God's vision of creation.

My Dog is a perfect example!

Much can be learned by my relationship with her! In terms of redefining sin as material separation from the spiritual energy of God, her behavior serves as a profound example of this balance in action.

Seemingly, she is at peace with her life and surroundings. Instinctively she lives in the moment. Her material needs—food, shelter, companionship—are straightforward, and she meets these needs without excessive attachment or greed. She seems content in a simple, joyful existence, while remaining connected to the flow of love and energy that unites us all with the divine. She doesn't dwell on the past or obsess over the future. She exists in the present moment, fully engaged with her surroundings and relationships.

In a way, she becomes a teacher and reminder of what salvation, or reconciliation with material needs and spiritual consciousness, can look like. She inspires me to explore how humans can learn to live more harmoniously within God's creation.

Even Self-indulgence is part of God's plan!

In humans, our day-to-day world places huge demands on our physical needs. Our very survival hinges on building relationships and careers to thrive and provide food and shelter. Emotions, ego, and self-interest are motivating forces that drive us to achieve those objectives. Because we are physical beings, it is not only proper but essential to focus on satisfying our daily needs to function and fulfill our purpose in this life.

Fulfilling our physical needs and desires is essential to fulfilling God's vision. Remember, God is everything! God exists both as the material world we see and as the eternal spiritual essence that connects us all. This view sees no separation between God and creation—every part of existence, from our physical bodies to the universe itself, is God expressing Himself in different forms.

In other words, creation isn't just made by God; it *is* God. So, attending to our physical needs is not a diversion from God's vision but an essential part of it. Because God IS us, manifesting Himself through us, fulfilling our needs and desires is God physically engaging with the material world through us, as a part of His creation.

The awesome beauty of God's plan is that He uses free will and choice as evolutionary tools to allow creation to naturally evolve. Just as an artist allows paint to mix and blend organically to create a masterpiece, God also allows creation to evolve without controlling every detail. This freedom expresses God's infinite creativity, manifesting through us as we navigate the balance between material and spiritual existence. By its nature, this evolutionary process requires material consumption to thrive. All things are consumed and then transformed into new manifestations of existence. This is how God continually evolves and expresses Himself.

The spirit of God needs to manifest in physical form!

God needs to 'feel' his creation! Without material evolution, the spiritual is incomplete. God's divine dream includes a profound yearning to manifest in material form, for without materiality, the spiritual feels unfulfilled. Guided by a grand design, the spiritual employs evolution as a means to freely unfold within a set of divine laws—laws that balance positive and negative events to foster growth and manifest infinite incarnations. These incarnations, each carrying an element of free will, evolve within the framework of divine rules, ensuring that creation eternally aligns with the spirit's conscious vision of love.

Even extremes are reconciled in God's plan!

If salvation lies in reconciling material desires with spiritual intent, even extreme cases of wrongdoing must align with this framework. These situations challenge our understanding of balance and push us to confront the relationship between personal consequences, communal impact, and the role of human free will in the divine plan.

Consider the example of Hitler—His actions embody an extreme distortion—a manifestation of material excess driven by the unchecked pursuit of domination and destruction. Yet, even such catastrophic imbalances play a role within God's evolutionary framework. They force humanity to respond, to create systems of justice, laws, and collective values that reinforce balance. The atrocities compel societies to examine their vulnerabilities, inspire the protection of human rights, and cultivate compassion. This communal reckoning becomes a step in the evolutionary process, ultimately serving God's plan by guiding creation toward greater harmony.

But what of Hitler himself? If the divine spirit is not fragmented into separate souls but is instead the singular, all-encompassing spirit of God, then his material existence represents a temporary distortion of that infinite love. When his life ends, the spirit within him, like all spirits, is released back into the eternal flow of divine love, free from material distortions. On a personal level, however, the consequences of his material excesses may manifest as profound shame or inner defeat—a self-destruction born from the hollowness of his existence. His material life, consumed by hatred and destruction, would have denied him any experience of peace, love, or connection. The ultimate "price" he pays is his inability to reconcile with these spiritual truths while alive, leaving his earthly existence as a shadow of what it could have been.

Now consider the billionaire—whose life revolves around accumulating and enjoying immense wealth. The Bible warns that, *'it is easier for a camel to pass through the eye of a needle than for a rich man*

to enter the kingdom of heaven.' This stark imagery speaks to the spiritual cost of excessive material desires. Extreme wealth often requires a deep focus on acquiring and maintaining it, inherently prioritizing material ambitions over spiritual awareness. While great wealth can provide societal benefits—creating jobs, funding innovation, and fostering economic growth—it also introduces systemic imbalances. The concentration of wealth can inspire collective responses, such as the formation of unions, progressive taxation, or social programs aimed at protecting the less fortunate and restoring societal equilibrium.

For the wealthy individual, however, the personal toll can be profound. Though material riches may bring comfort and happiness, they often come at the expense of spiritual fulfillment. The relentless pursuit of wealth can foster detachment from the interconnected spirit of love that permeates all creation. This disconnection leaves the individual spiritually hollow, less generous, and unable to fully appreciate the richness of existence beyond their possessions. In contrast, those with less material wealth often demonstrate greater generosity, perhaps because their lives are less encumbered by the distractions of excessive material desires. Their connection to the divine spirit often shines through in acts of love, community, and gratitude.

Ultimately, wealth itself is not inherently virtuous or corrupt. Its value is determined by the balance an individual strikes between material indulgence and spiritual awareness. The billionaire who uses their wealth to uplift others and connect with the greater good may still find harmony. But for those consumed by their riches, the price is a life out of balance—an existence filled with material pleasures but devoid of the spiritual connection that brings true fulfillment.

What about the disabled person—who appears unable to contribute materially to the world—those confined to a bed, unable to move or speak? What role do they play in God's creation? It's tempting to see such lives as purposeless, but that perspective dismisses the profound ways they may influence others. Their existence, like all manifestations, is infused with divine purpose. Their existence may inspire medical advancements or awaken compassion in others. On a personal level, they could manifest love and gratitude so, even in such unimaginable circumstances, they become examples serving as reminders of the indomitable human spirit and the infinite ways God's presence can inspire others to live their best life.

On the other hand, what if they just succumb to despair or bitterness? Even then, they may inspire an even deeper compassion and sense of purpose among family, friends and caregivers. Their personal toll might be unnecessary emotional suffering that results from failing to embrace love or purpose in their circumstances. So even then, their material existence, while challenging, still offers opportunities to reflect God's spirit through endurance, gratitude, or connection.

Moral flaws cannot disrupt God's plan!

Believing that God is everything brings a reassuring perspective: moral flaws are anomalies of evolution, not disruptions of the divine plan. Since God encompasses all and is guided by love, events that would irreparably undermine the divine vision cannot occur. Our material lives are imbued with burdens—be they power, wealth, suffering, or indulgence. Each burden carries the potential to either distort or reflect the divine spirit within us. The personal consequences for imbalances— be it shame, hollowness, or unnecessary suffering—are inevitable, as they are intrinsic to the material experience. Yet, the communal benefits can be equally profound. Each individual's choices ripple outward, shaping societies, values, and the collective spiritual journey of humanity.

Ultimately, the divine spirit's infinite love provides the framework for these experiences, allowing free will to guide the material world. While excesses and imbalances are permitted, they are not without cost—either to the individual or to the collective. However, it is the intrinsic human desire for moral righteousness, for justice, and for connection that serves as a natural guardrail against indulgence. This yearning, rooted in the divine spirit itself, compels us toward balance, reminding us that salvation lies not in perfection but in the ongoing reconciliation of our material and spiritual selves.

So, Salvation is a uniquely human need!

The rest of nature seems to exist effortlessly within the balance of the spiritual and the material. I see this so clearly on my daily walks with my dog. Watching her, I'm struck by how she is completely in the moment. Her world is centered on the sensations around her—sniffing every blade of grass, following her instincts with focus and curiosity. She doesn't worry about where we're going or what comes next. She recognizes our path, but she has no concept of the concrete sidewalk beneath her paws or that it was carefully designed by humans to organize our towns into logical grids of neighborhoods.

She doesn't know the cars passing by are machines we've built to move us from place to place or that the houses and stores along the route are structures we've created to house our lives and commerce. She doesn't think about how we grow, harvest, and process food or how money facilitates all of it. All she knows is that we're together. She trusts the universe will provide her with what she needs: food when she's hungry, shelter when she's tired, and the comfort of my companionship. She exists in a state of natural balance—spiritual and material, instinctively aligned with her purpose in life.

This simplicity reminds me of the biblical words: *"Look at the birds of the air; they neither sow nor reap nor gather into barns, and yet your heavenly Father feeds them."* The birds—and my dog—are part of nature's design, functioning as they were meant to, without over thinking or overcomplicating their existence.

Humans, on the other hand, are a different story. We possess incredible cognitive abilities—abilities to reason, create, and build systems that make life easier and more meaningful. These gifts, however, also come with a cost. The same intellect that drives innovation also tempts us toward greed, overindulgence, and the relentless pursuit of power. We are constantly distracted by material desires, losing sight of our spiritual purpose.

Unlike the rest of nature, we need to actively pursue balance. Through meditation, prayer, or other practices of reflection, we attempt to reconcile the material and spiritual aspects of our lives. This conscious effort to realign ourselves is what I understand as salvation—not a promise of something in the afterlife but a process of bringing our lives into harmony with the divine vision in the here and now.

Material needs dominate spiritual selves!

It's natural for the demands of our material selves to overpower our spiritual selves. Our material selves require satisfaction of physical needs to exist, while our spiritual selves provide discernment for making balanced decisions. Although our bodies are temporary and our spirits are eternal, focusing on our physical needs is as vital to fulfilling God's plan as connecting to our spiritual selves. Material desires are not wrong—they are necessary. But they tend to dominate our priorities and often lead to excess and overindulgence. The more we are preoccupied with material desires, the more disconnected we become from spiritual awareness.

For example: What about Love vs. Desire—In our culture, physical attraction, or the pursuit of sex, often obscures our vision in ways that we misinterpret as the pursuit of love. True connection—the kind that might find divine love in a 'soulmate' style relationship—requires a deeper spiritual connection with the other person, not merely as a source of gratification. Salvation here lies in recognizing, and controlling these impulses in ways that allow spiritual guidance to help us see the spiritual essence within our partners and elevate love above physical desire.

The challenge is to maintain balance!

Our spiritual selves keep our material selves connected to God's vision of creation. Spiritual guidance comes through reflection, prayer, meditation, or quiet introspection. It often presents itself as inner clarity, a nudge toward compassion, or a sense of alignment with the greater good. To ensure our actions align with God's vision, we must reflect on questions like: *Is this action driven by love or fear? Does this choice serve others as well as myself?* This kind of introspection keeps us grounded in spiritual wisdom.

Understanding salvation as a balance between the material and the spiritual is one thing; living it is another. It's in the quiet, ordinary moments of life that I've found the clearest path to this balance. One of the most profound teachers in my spiritual journey has been my dog. Through her, I've learned how to move beyond reflection and into daily practice.

Here's how it works for me in my daily life!

For me, this process is as simple as walking with my dog. During these moments, I reflect on the day ahead, considering how to better anticipate the needs of others, question my instincts, and evaluate my responses.

It always begins by sensing that busyness in mind. To quiet my thoughts I try to forget everything and focus on the actions of my dog. She's just happy walking with me, connected with me, tuned into every action, sniffing a million different scents along our path that tell her where she is, who's been there, leaving her scent along the way. Eager to greet neighbors and get a pet on her head. Just experiencing the now with no thought for what might be coming the rest of the day. She's totally present in the material world and at the same time spiritually at peace. She reminds me that the only truly important thing is now. To live in the moment because that's all we have.

Now in a more peaceful state of mind I allow myself to reflect on the day. More aware now of the tensions within me. More conscious of the emotions and desires that motivate me I begin to seek spiritual influence to guide my actions.

Typically I begin by reminding myself I am not separate but connected to everything. I am me, my dog, the people I meet, the trees, the sky, the universe. All of us and everything is God in us. I look at my hands and realize I am just one of the tools in God's infinite number of manifestations. I tell my dog to sit and stare into her beautiful brown eyes, feeling her spirit, connecting with her spirit, recognizing her spirit as God staring back at me and bonding with my spirit. As people walk by I no longer see them as separate individuals, but as God within them as God is in me. I feel the living energy flowing through the trees and grass and sense the same energy of God flowing through them is the same river of energy flowing through me. I'm connected to all of God's creation.

In this way, seeing myself in everything gives me a new insight as to what it means to *'treat others as you would want to be treated'*. I begin to challenge my intentions for the day. Asking myself questions like: *Have I listened to others with my heart? Do I understand their wants and needs? Am I being fair and acting with love? How might I be more effective in my actions?* By thoughtfully weighing my options, I align my actions with my spiritual self, keeping connected to the divine spirit in everything I do.

This balance brings a sense of Salvation in that I've reconciled my material interests with my spiritual self. It makes me feel better about my choices and more confident I'm doing the right thing as I navigate the day ahead. I love and appreciate everything more.

Even the walk with my dog becomes more enjoyable!

Humanities Place in the Universe!

In the grand scheme of eternity, it's worth noting humans have only existed for less than the blink of an eye in the endless evolution of God's cosmic plan. As amazing, inspired and important to God as we think we are, we will eventually become extinct. All the wisdom, everything we've written, invented or ever done will vanish as if it never existed and be consumed by the eternal evolution of the universe. Yet, within this moment, we have the unique opportunity to embody divine presence, to live as conscious manifestations of the spirit of God.

The impermanence of humanity does not diminish our purpose; it elevates it. Each moment we live in balance, each choice guided by love and understanding, adds to the eternal cosmic display of God's creation.

Achieving Salvation is very simple!

It doesn't require making promises, seeking forgiveness or intense regret and restitution for wrongdoing. It's simply a matter of, on a daily basis, keeping aware of our human tendencies toward overindulging our material desires and seeking connection with our spiritual selves to maintain balance in our decisions. This keeps us aligned with acting out our lives in ways that best fulfill our purpose in our current incarnation of God's plan.

Walking with my dog each day reminds me that salvation isn't found in extraordinary acts or profound revelations but in the simple, mindful choices that align us with the divine. When we embrace our connection to everything—our neighbor, the trees, the stars—we transcend the limitations of our fleeting existence.

And so, my dog teaches me, salvation isn't a destination or a prize. It's a way of walking through life—connected, mindful, and at peace. By observing and meditating on my relationship with her I've learned connecting with God can be as simple as... **"Praying With Your Dog!"**

CHAPTER
SIX

Heaven

**HEAVEN IS
ALL AROUND US!**

6 | HEAVEN

"We're already in heaven!"

Heaven is all around us! It's everywhere we look! All we have to do is see it, feel it, connect with it, be part of it!

Look up at the night sky. See the billions of stars, the moon, imagine ourselves so tiny in relation to it all. Think of the infinite possibilities in the universe. Feel that mysterious life energy flowing through us. As I stand here with my dog sitting quietly at my side, taking it all in with me, I imagine the same energy flowing through me that's flowing through her. We're connected by the energy of love.

And I sense that same magical, mystical energy flowing through everything around us. The trees, the frogs croaking, the crickets chirping. And I imagine that same energy that's connecting all of this as the same energy penetrating the awesome power of the infinite universe, holding everything together through gravitational, electromagnetic and other mysterious energy forces my mind can't even conceive of. All of this is awesomely connected and working together in an eternal evolutionary divine plan infinitely manifesting itself in unimaginable ways!

If this isn't heaven on display right before our eyes, I don't know what is! If we don't stand in awe at this spectacle, and be humbled and thankful to be part of this blessing we are missing the miracle in our midst. God isn't hiding from us, God is revealing his awesome creation in all its glory for us to see, and feel, and touch! When we open our eyes to this we realize we are already in heaven. It's just up to us to embrace it, join it, be part of it, live it.

But while these ideas resonate with me, they conflict with some of the fundamental Christian views of Heaven I was brought up with.

Heaven promised or Heaven now?

Some believe heaven is yet to come. But for me, this idea doesn't fit with my vision of what heaven means to me.

They dream of a paradise that God is preparing for those who are saved. It would be a new earth, just like the one we are living in but with none of the bad things. We're joined by our loved ones, including our pets. Everything would be perfect. We'll all live in perfect happiness and harmony. Everyone equally provided for with no want, evil, hunger, sickness or sadness. And we live with Jesus and walk with God for eternity.

I'm not saying anyone is wrong for believing this because who am I to say my way is right? Admittedly, it is a beautiful vision. I totally understand why people love this idea. And for those that do, it's a very good thing because I'm sure many are motivated to live Godly lives to achieve it. In a way, I envy those who can believe this because it sounds very nice and I would love to go there. But in my honest heart of hearts, my soul tells me it's not right. There are just too many questions and it strikes me as a materially focused view of heaven that doesn't work for me.

For example... if we are physically resurrected, how old will we be? Are we all the same age, not too young, not too old? If so, how will we recognize those who were decades different in age when we knew them? Are the houses, or rooms, that we live in all the same? If so, does that mean we no longer get to choose the living style we like? Do we get to enjoy eating food? If so, don't animals have to die so we can eat? Will we be able to pursue different talents? Or are we stuck with the talents we had in life? Are the answers to these questions; *we will simply live in a divine state and none of this will matter?* If so, how does that match up with the idea; *everything will be just like it is now but with none of the bad things?* I could go on but this conveys the idea about why there are too many questions.

But the biggest problem I have with all this is, although they speak of heaven in a spiritual sense, the real emphasis seems to be on looking forward to the material rewards. In other words, what happens if you take away the idea that we are bodily resurrected, and what if we don't get to be with our loved ones or our material needs are not met? If you take away those promises, what happens to people's faith?

I mean, what if the idea of receiving heavenly rewards didn't exist? What if Jesus never existed? Would we lose our faith in God? What then would happen to our motivation for living a godly life? Shouldn't we want to live that way just because it's the right way to live?

So heaven isn't coming, it's here now!

Even if Jesus never existed, I would still believe in Jesus! And here's why. Heaven isn't about achieving eternal life through salvation by the literal blood sacrifice of the lamb of God. The true power of the story of Jesus is about how the spirit of God manifested in human form to demonstrate how humankind, by living in balance with spiritual awareness, as humans we can fulfill God's divine purpose for creation. The story of Jesus represents the constant resurrection of the eternal spirit over physical death. In other words, the spirit never dies, but the physical is temporary. Living our lives balanced by spiritual purpose keeps us connected to God.

This view challenges me to think more deeply about how my vision of heaven fits with the nature of God and how it might relate to a deeper understanding of the spiritual focus of Jesus' teachings. About how God revealed his spirit in human form to demonstrate how we can live our best life to fulfill God's divine plan. Teachings that remind us God is Love and how the spirit of love conquers all over temporary human desires. And about how achieving daily reconciliation of these imbalances keeps us connected to God who resides in eternal heaven. Knowing God in this way keeps us in a state of grace where God reveals heaven to us every day.

Heaven is the realization 'Love is God!'

It almost sounds trite when I say 'God is Love' because everybody says it! But I've come to a new, much deeper, understanding of what that means. And once I did grasp the true essence of that statement it changed my life forever. To get there, I first needed to realize the power of Love is something much more awesome than anything I had ever previously imagined. It totally redefined what the word 'Love' means to me.

In fact, this single idea became the inspiration for this entire book! It came to me from an experience of sitting with my dog and meditating on this feeling of love which felt like an energy flowing between us. I became curious about the essence of that energy. As I prayed upon it more I sensed it flowing through nature all around us. I began to think of it as something much greater than simply an emotion but actually a spiritual force that was the essential energy binding all of existence. This inspired my journey to discover God in powerful ways that compelled me to write this book.

It began not by thinking 'God is Love', but rather that 'Love is God'! It became a new realization that 'Love' is much greater than just an emotion. It's actually a living, powerful, magical, mysterious energy force that not only penetrates, but binds all of creation. It's the living presence of God expressing itself in an infinite number of ways. It's the spiritual energy of God fueling the energy of our souls and guides the manifestation of God's cosmic dream of creation.

So, heaven isn't coming some day, it's already here! It's all around us! God's 'love' is the eternal spiritual energy that flows through us and everything. It's in us, and outside of us, and on display before our very eyes. It's the same magical, mysterious, spiritual energy that binds the positive and negative charges contained in all atoms which form all of material existence. An energy that is the essence of God present in all matter. It's me, my dog, you, the trees, the birds, the bees, the sky, the sun, the moon, the stars, our galaxy, the universe, the entire cosmos of God's infinite creation. The conscious energy of God guiding the free evolution of the cosmos as it manifests to fulfill God's divine vision of creation.

Everything is the expression of God!

How can words ever capture the essence of God, or Love? No language holds the depth to fully express the divine. God encompasses all—both the spiritual and the material. The spirit of God finds its completeness in the physical manifestation of the universe, and we, as humans, are part of that fulfillment. Through our being, our love, and the way we live our lives, we express the essence of God.

But we are not the sole fulfillment of God's longing to feel and experience creation. All of existence—every tree, every star, every creature, every atom—joins in this divine expression. Each is another way God experiences the wonder and beauty of an infinite, evolving creation. Together, all things manifest the divine dream, intertwining to form the kingdom of God revealed. Our lives, along with all of creation, are an invitation to experience heaven here and now—for all who open their hearts to recognize it.

Heaven is all around us!

I think of this every time I go for a walk with my dog! I almost feel like I'm taking a deep breath and breathing it all in as I think of it! The awesome wonder of it all, what I'm seeing, thinking and feeling, leaves me astounded and feeling blessed to know I get to play a part in this.

When we imagine heaven, it's easy to dream of something disconnected from the world we know—a perfect place waiting beyond. But creation itself reveals a profound truth: heaven isn't something apart; it's embedded in the integrated, evolving systems of the universe, from the microscopic to the cosmic.

At the micro level, life depends on systems we can't even see. Inside the soil, microbes form vast, interconnected networks that sustain plants by breaking down nutrients and sharing resources. In turn, plants provide energy to these microbes, creating a mutually beneficial system. Similarly, the human microbiome—trillions of microbes within us—helps digest food, regulate health, and keep our bodies functioning. These systems thrive not in isolation but through cooperation, illustrating how even the smallest components of life are part of something greater.

Zoom out, and we see this same interconnectedness in nature. A forest is not a collection of isolated trees but an integrated network. Trees communicate and share nutrients through the mycelium beneath the soil, a vast fungal network often called nature's internet. Animals, insects, plants, and fungi form a web of interdependence, cycling energy and resources to maintain the balance of ecosystems. Seasons evolve predictably, ensuring renewal and growth, further highlighting nature's cooperative design.

At the grandest scale, the cosmos reflects this same order. Planets orbit stars, galaxies interact, and gravitational forces maintain balance. What appears chaotic—exploding stars or swirling galaxies—follows precise laws that ensure the universe's stability and growth. Even the smallest variations in physical constants would render existence impossible, but instead, everything operates in harmony, like an orchestra playing a divine composition.

Taken together, these layers of creation—microbial, biological, and the cosmic universe—show a pattern of interconnectedness and evolution. They remind us that heaven is not a static place but an integrated state of divine order. Just as microbes, forests, and galaxies evolve while remaining balanced within larger systems, so too does the divine creation we are part of.

When we imagine heaven, let us consider it in the context of how creation already works. Heaven isn't something distant or separate; it's an unfolding reality embedded in the systems of life and the cosmos. It is here, now, evolving alongside us, just as God intended.

Heaven is everything we say, think and do!

While the natural world and cosmos reveal a profound interconnectedness, humanity adds its own unique layers to the picture of heaven. Through our creative expressions, acts of compassion, and the joy we find in life's simple moments, we reflect the divine presence in ways that enrich and elevate creation itself.

Consider the power of creative expression. Art, in its many forms, offers glimpses of heaven by connecting us to something greater than ourselves. A painting can stir emotions we didn't know were there; music can evoke joy, sorrow, or awe, transcending language and culture. Creative inventions, from the tools that simplify daily life to technologies that solve complex challenges, demonstrate humanity's capacity to improve the world through ingenuity and inspiration. These acts of creation mirror the divine act of creation itself, showing that humanity is not separate from but deeply integrated into the ongoing work of the divine.

Beyond creation, there's the joy we find in human experience. Watching a child explore the world with wonder and curiosity reminds us of life's boundless possibilities. Sharing in another's happiness or pride in their accomplishments brings a sense of unity and shared purpose. These moments are not fleeting pleasures; they are reflections of the joy and harmony that define heaven.

And then there's compassion and goodwill—the quiet acts of kindness that transform the ordinary into the sacred. A helping hand extended to a stranger, a word of encouragement to someone in need, or simply showing empathy to another person—all of these demonstrate the divine love that flows through humanity. When we act with kindness, we don't just improve the world around us; we participate in the divine order, weaving the human spirit into the larger tapestry of creation.

Together, these expressions of humanity—our creativity, joy, compassion, and goodwill—are not separate from the interconnected systems of the natural world or the cosmos. Instead, they add depth and dimension to the picture of heaven already present in creation. Humanity's role in this grand design is not to dominate but to contribute, to reflect the divine through our unique gifts and shared experiences.

In these ways, we show that heaven is not just something we find in the natural world or the vastness of the cosmos; it is also something we create and nurture within ourselves and each other. Heaven exists wherever there is beauty, joy, and love—wherever humanity mirrors the divine spirit in thought, action, and heart.

Dreams Are a Window to Heaven!

Consider our dreams. Often, I wake in that space between asleep and awake, confused about where I am—drifting between a desire to remain in my dream and the pull of conscious awareness drawing me back to this reality. I try to hold on to that dream space, yearning to resolve the experience, to stay with the people I was interacting with. Yet as my mind awakens to the day, no matter how hard I try to hold on, the dream slips away like a snowflake melting in my hand.

But it felt so real! I was surrounded by friends, family, my dogs, and even others I don't know. I reunited with those I've lost—my father, mother, grandparents, and dogs. Even long-lost friends have come to me, people I've not seen for years. I could do fantastic things that seem impossible in my waking world: flying, leaping between buildings, and visiting familiar places that felt like home, only to see them transform into deeper, symbolic reflections of what they mean to me. I've seen colors so vivid and pure they seem beyond reality. I've found myself in two places at once or outside myself, watching myself. Sometimes, I've even become someone else or communicated directly with animals.

In all these dream adventures, I remain grounded in who I am. My experiences in the dream world don't erase my waking identity—they expand it. I've come to believe dreams are not merely dreams; they are real, just as real as the life we experience in this material world.

Our bodies are material; they need rest. But our spirits are eternal and never sleep. While our daily lives demand focus on material needs, sleep allows our spirits to roam. When our bodies rest, our spirits are freed from the demands of consciousness to explore other dimensions of existence. Yet, because our bodies still require their connection to the eternal energy that sustains us, our spirits remain tethered, grounded in this reality. This tether allows us to experience incredible, otherworldly events while maintaining our bond to the here and now.

Dreams, then, are a window into heaven, a glimpse into a dimension far more awesome than our waking minds can comprehend. When loved ones visit us in dreams, these are not mere figments of memory but real interactions. Our dreams are God's way of opening a doorway, showing us that our spirits remain united, even beyond physical life.

Dreams are proof of eternal connection—proof that there is no spiritual death. When our material bodies cease to function, like all things in nature, they transform and manifest in new ways. But our spiritual consciousness endures as part of the eternal spirit of God. All that we are—our memories, emotions, and love—joins with the rest of creation, contributing to the divine plan and remaining forever connected.

Heaven Is Beyond Our Imagination!

Heaven is everything and more! It encompasses the entire universe, the human experience, and realms beyond our comprehension. Since the dawn of humanity, we've sought the divine and the meaning of life. Theologians interpret sacred texts; philosophers delve into human behavior and morality; scientists explore the origins of the universe and questions of infinity.

Though their pursuits differ, all these paths converge in shared curiosity about existence's grand design. And as enlightened as we believe ourselves to be, despite all our prayers, studies, and discoveries, the answers to creation's mystery will always elude us. No single species, no matter how advanced, will ever comprehend the entirety of the divine plan.

Yet, we can know this: together, we are God living in heaven. Individually, we are blessed to be part of it.

Love is All There Is!

One of the greatest mysteries that has puzzled humankind for thousands of years is the question: where does consciousness come from? Many, even within the scientific community, suggest that the origins of the universe may be linked to this enigma. Yet, as compelling as this idea may be, my journey over the past few years has led me to a different conclusion. I don't believe consciousness holds the ultimate answer. Instead, I've come to believe that *love* is the source of everything. Love is not merely an emotion or an abstract ideal—*Love IS God*. Everything emanates from love.

Think about it: Love is an emotion, but I believe it is the only true emotion. All other emotions arise as extensions of love. For example:

- *Happiness* is receiving something you love.
- *Sadness* is not having something you love.
- *Anger* is when love is taken from you.
- *Hate* is the distortion or rejection of love.
- *Sympathy* is caring for something you love.

At its core, love is the desire that fuels all emotional responses. As Kahlil Gibran eloquently states in *The Prophet*, *"Love has no other desire but to fulfill itself."*

Love's intrinsic desire to fulfill its dreams is the fuel that drives all existence. Our love for comfort, companionship, and discovery motivates us to work, create families, and pursue creative endeavors. In nature, the instinctual behaviors that support procreation and evolutionary processes reflect a similar force—a driving energy that sustains life. Many animals and even plants exhibit behaviors that resemble the protective and nurturing qualities of human love.

Love as the Primordial Force!

Contrary to the notion that consciousness might be the fundamental force underlying creation, I've come to see emotion—and specifically love—as the primary force from which consciousness emerges. Consider what compels us to act. It isn't merely awareness of our surroundings but an emotional desire to achieve, protect, or connect. This desire drives the processes of evolution and creation. Consciousness, on the other hand, acts as a tool—a mechanism that allows us to perceive love, navigate, interpret, and respond to our experiences. It's as though consciousness operates like a series of light switches, illuminating varying levels of awareness tailored to the unique needs of each species. But it is love—the single driving emotion—that powers the machinery of existence.

If love is the source of all creation, then Love is God. And how do I know this? Because I *feel* it. If I can feel this energy, and if I'm conscious of it, then I know God feels it too. Love is as tangible as anything I can see or touch. It pulses through me like a spiritual energy, connecting

147

me with everything—my family, friends, and the world around me. Love is what makes life meaningful and vibrant. It's a mysterious, divine force, flowing through every aspect of existence. Love is the singular energy that binds all things, an eternal spirit connecting the material and the spiritual, the alpha and the omega of existence.

We never really die!

Through this understanding, I've come to believe we never truly die; we are eternally transformed. Love, the eternal spirit that infuses all creation, is the force that binds us to God's infinite desire to fulfill itself—a celestial dream of creation that is boundless and unending.

Just as all matter in the universe transforms, so do we. Our bodies, composed of trillions of atomic particles, return to the earth when the spirit departs, dissipating like dust to dust, only to become part of new evolutions of God's creation. We are no different than a flower that blooms, fades, and falls, only to nourish the soil that brings forth new life. In this endless cycle, we, too, are re-woven into the fabric of existence, becoming part of the eternal unfolding of God's vision.

And yet, while our physical forms return to the earth, our souls are released from the tether of this material existence. All that we are—our awareness, talents, knowledge, memories, and love—remains connected to the eternal soul of God. Our spiritual energies join the collective consciousness, enriching the infinite dream of creation.

Our souls are like a river, winding its way through the mountains of life, gathering experiences, connections, and love along its journey. When the river reaches the ocean, it does not cease to exist; it becomes one with the vast, infinite waters. It is still everything the river was, but it is now part of something greater—boundless, eternal, and whole. Likewise, when we merge with the spiritual essence of God, we carry with us the pure love and blessings of this lifetime. Forever connected to the souls we've known and the love we've shared, we are ready to embark on the next manifestation of existence, united in the eternal flow of divine creation.

So, there is no need to fear death. Just as we entered this world at birth—innocent and unaware of what was to come— we will transition from this life into the next with the same divine grace. At birth, we carried no premonitions or promises, no memories of the soulmates we had known before. And yet, we embraced this life with wonder, curiosity, and an adventurous spirit, eager for all it had to offer. We pursued dreams, experienced love, built relationships, and shared in the profound beauty of existence.

Our bodies serve us as vessels for this journey, allowing us to explore, create, and connect. When they are no longer needed, our spirit is released, carrying with it all the love, memories, and experiences of this lifetime.

These treasures become part of the eternal soul of God, enriching the collective consciousness and preparing us for the next evolution of our existence in God's infinite plan. Death is not an ending; it is a continuation of the divine flow, a return to the source from which we came, and the beginning of yet another chapter in the boundless story of creation.

Love defies definition. It can never be measured or quantified because it is pure divine energy that has no form or material properties. It is the eternal spirit of God, the singular source of energy that sustains and animates all existence. Through love, we are already part of heaven. It is not a distant place but a reality woven into our daily lives. Love is forever unfolding in an infinite evolution of God's dream of creation.

So my journey comes full circle.

As I write the closing to this book, I find myself back where I started—sitting on the doorstep with my dog lying peacefully at my feet. I wonder what's going through her mind as we share this quiet moment, love flowing effortlessly between us.

Five years ago, when this journey began, I never imagined I would write a book about it. But each step led me to places of spiritual awakening so profound, I felt compelled to capture them. Year by year, page by page, I felt as though I was discovering God for the first time.

This path of discovery challenged the foundations of my upbringing and revealed truths undeniable to my soul. Through meditation and prayer, new concepts of God unfolded within me, as if whispered by an inner knowing. To my amazement, these ideas often aligned with teachings from theology, philosophy, and science— affirming their resonance.

At its core, my discovery is this: <u>Love is God, and all existence—spiritual and material—is one in the infinite spirit of Love.</u>

In the end, I've come to a simple truth: Finding God is a deeply personal journey. It doesn't require theological expertise or scientific knowledge. For thousands of years, great thinkers have illuminated the way, but no teacher, preacher, or book can give you the answers. There is no single right path or absolute truth. All that's needed is a sincere heart and the courage to seek. As the scriptures say, *"Seek, and ye shall find."*

Finally, here I am, still sitting with my dog, feeling the love between us and the divine presence that connects us. I am blessed to know God more deeply than ever before, simply by looking into nature with open eyes and a prayerful heart.

So, if you're wondering where to begin your journey,
I leave you with this humble suggestion:
"Pray with your dog!"

ABOUT THE AUTHOR
Garrett Walker

For nearly five years, I have been immersed in the writing of this book—a journey sparked by quiet moments spent with my beloved golden retriever. As I sat pondering the unspoken thoughts of my dog and basked in the undeniable bond of love between us, I found myself drawn toward profound questions about the nature of God. This journey led to an extraordinary revelation: Love is God. This book is the result of that discovery—a deeply personal exploration of divine connection, inspired by the simple yet profound relationship I shared with a loyal companion.

Professionally, I began my career as an art director and creative director. I went on to establish and lead a successful marketing and creative services agency, crafting campaigns for Fortune 500 consumer products companies. It was in this role I honed my skills as both a professional artist and writer, developing my ability to communicate ideas with clarity and creativity.

Throughout my life, golden retrievers have played an integral role, guiding and inspiring me in unexpected ways. My third dog, Honey Bear, became the muse for this book—a gentle soul whose presence encouraged deep introspection and spiritual growth. In Honey Bear's company, I found a space to reflect on life's biggest questions and ultimately to redefine my understanding of God.

Raised in a fundamentalist Christian family, I was instilled with a deep reverence for spiritual matters from an early age. However, my curiosity and desire for a more nuanced understanding of faith led me to explore esoteric and unconventional perspectives. This lifelong quest for spiritual meaning culminated in the insights shared within this book.

Writing this book has been nothing short of transformative for me. It has provided me with an entirely new perspective on the divine and a profound sense of connection with the living spirit of God. For the first time, I feel a genuine, personal relationship with the divine—a truth I felt compelled to share. Originally written with friends and family in mind, the book is now offered to anyone seeking a deeper, more personal connection with God.

I hope this work serves as a guide and inspiration, offering readers a fresh lens through which to view their own relationship with the divine. Above all, I hope it reminds others that God's love is as close and accessible as the loyal companion by your side.

www.ingramcontent.com/pod-product-compliance
Lightning Source LLC
Chambersburg PA
CBHW060207070426
42447CB00035B/2819